THE TAO OF JESUS

An Experiment in Inter-Traditional Understanding

·

Joseph A. Loya, O.S.A.

Wan-Li Ho

Chang-Shin Jih

PAULIST PRESS
New York/Mahwah, N.J.

Cover design by Cindy Dunne

•

Interior design by Joseph E. Petta

•

Copyright © 1998 by Joseph A. Loya

•

•

Library of Congress Cataloging-in-Publication Data

Loya, Joseph A.
The Tao of Jesus : an experiment in inter-traditional understanding / Joseph A. Loya, Wan-Li Ho, Chang-Shin Jih.
p.   cm.
Includes bibliographical references.
ISBN 0-8091-3764-X (alk. paper)
1. Christianity and other religions—Taoism. 2. Taoism—Relations—Christianity. I. Ho, Wan-Li. II. Jih, Chang-Shin. III. Title.
BR128.T34L69   1998
261.2´9514—dc21   97-45162
                                                                                            CIP

•

Published by Paulist Press
997 Macarthur Boulevard
Mahwah, New Jersey 07430

www.paulistpress.com

Printed and bound in the
United States of America

CONTENTS.

PERMISSIONS.

THE AUTHORS.

Joseph A. Loya, O.S.A., is an associate professor in the theology and religious studies department at Villanova University. He holds a Ph.D. in the history of Christianity, and is an active participant in the ecumenical movement on the national level.

Wan-Li Ho has served as an adjunct faculty member in the department of humanities and communications at Drexel University. Her book comparing the worldviews of *Ecclesiastes* and Chuang Tzu is in its second printing in Taiwan.

Chang-Shin (Luke) Jih, lectures in the field of comparative philosophy and interreligious dialogue, is a certified Taoist priest, and also instructs in a body-mind empowerment program that is rooted in Taoist principles.

ARTWORK.

Within the world of Chinese art, it would be difficult to overestimate the impact and stature of Yu Peng (b. 1955). He has gained an international reputation as one who infuses new life into artistic codes that have become tired and clichéd. His lines are agitated, tension-filled, and charged with an explosive energy, but always under a command of spirit that harmonizes the incompatibilities and evokes order out of the chaos.

DEDICATED TO THE MEMORY

OF

PROFESSOR CHARLES WEI-HSUN FU (1933–1996)

•

FOUNTAIN OF VITALITY

PHILOSOPHER

PUBLIC INTELLECTUAL

PROLIFIC WRITER

EDUCATOR

BUILDER OF BRIDGES
BETWEEN WESTERN AND ASIAN THOUGHT

ACKNOWLEDGMENTS.

This book would not have been realized without the encouragement, guidance, support, and professional watch and ward of Bernard Prusak, Sandra Wawrytko, Leonard Swidler, Reverend John Loya, Yu Peng, Eva Gibson, and Randy Rolfe.

Our hearts are filled with gratitude.

INTRODUCTION.

In no way does this work present itself as an attempt to pull Christian rabbits out of Taoist hats, to adapt a Thomas Merton disclaimer of felicitous phrasing. Rather, this book intends to evoke the kind of delight that arises when something familiar is apprehended in what was formerly thought to be completely alien to oneself. The "self" in this case could be (A) a mature, reflective, critically thinking and committed Christian reading words that Taoists attribute to Lao Tzu and Chuang Tzu, (B) a Taoist counterpart reading words that Christians attribute to Jesus, or (C) any interested observer of cultural history who is readily edified by instances that demonstrate cross-cultural connections.

Leo Lefebure, in reviewing occasions of mutual enrichment experienced by participants in Christian–Buddhist encounters of late, concluded that it is only after realizing that the two traditions are not the same can we venture to see ways in which they may not be different.[1] The fact that Christianity and Taoism are not the same—are ultimately irreducible to each other—is undeniable. Philosophical Taoism does not admit of a personal creator-deity who is source of life and object of devotion. Elements of Christian life and thought such as prayer, sin, grace, redemption or salvation cannot be transposed into the life and thought of philosophical Taoism without the near dissolution of their original meanings. Christian mystical experience presupposes an immutable transcendent reality and a contingent but real world, whereas Taoism holds to an "intraworldly" mysticism that aims to see this one-and-only existing world in a new way.[2] A Christian preacher who attempts to deliver a sermon based on the Taoistic transmoral system of "no good, no evil, no right, no wrong," would no doubt leave the members of the congregation thoroughly confounded rather than spiritually edified.

This having been said, what then can be gained from the thematic juxtaposition of locutions attributed to foundational figures representing a transcendental religion on one hand, and what can be described as a philosophy of simple but profound naturalism on the other? Justification for this effort rests upon the following basis: Christian and Taoist worldviews represent an example of the kind of polarities that should be linked whenever and however possible in accord with the recommendation of a growing number of learned, historically conscious commentators on the human condition. Appropriate here is a reference to Professor Ashok Gangadean's contention that the world is now witnessing the struggle between two competing paradigms or models of what it means to be human—the struggle between the egocentric view of humanness and the emerging dialogical human being. He writes:

"While egocentric culture leads increasingly to separations, divisions, strife and polarizations in aspects of human life, the emerging dialogical consciousness enhances communication, compassion, mutual nurturing and care for others....Awakening to this dialogical advance affects every aspect of our life: our inner well-being, our relations with others, our capacity to negotiate fundamental differences in our shared cultural space, our ability to honor and cultivate the human and natural ecology....It becomes clear that interreligious dialogue is at the very core of this dialogical turn...the passage from the egocentric life to the dialogical life takes courage, since to truly open one's self dialogically to the other calls for the deepest transformation in how we exist: how we truly open to others who live in different worlds, in very different perspectives."[3]

Ewert Cousins calls such creative encounters "dialogic dialogue," as distinguished from "dialectical dialogue," in which one tries to refute the claims of the other. The outcome of the former kind of dialogue is not victory or failure for one of the partners, but a "complexified consciousness" for all as the parties in dialogue are "mutually enriched by passing over into the consciousness of the other so that each can experience the other's values from within the other's perspective."[4] Because noth-

2

ing is negated that should not be negated in one's own or the other's tradition, this will be a truly complexified global consciousness, not a mere universal, undifferentiated, abstract consciousness.

Leonard Swidler affirms:

"All this of course will have to be done with complete integrity on each side, each partner remaining authentically true to the vital core of his/her own religious tradition. However, in significant ways that vital core will be perceived and experienced differently under the influence of the dialogue, but, if the dialogue is carried on with both integrity and openness the result will be that, for example, the Jew will be authentically Jewish and the Christian will be authentically Christian....There can be no talk of a syncretism here, for syncretism means amalgamating various elements of different religions into kind of a (con)fused whole without concern for the integrity of the religions involved—which is not the case with authentic dialogue."[5]

There is no illusion among such scholars as to the critical nature of establishing a commitment to dialogue and the formation of a global consciousness in these times of mounting tensions and threats on small planet earth: "It is an absolute necessity," writes Cousins, "if we are to survive."[6]

Decades before the above thoughts were composed, the aforementioned Merton, a Christian monk who immersed himself in the religious/philosophical imagination of the Orient, stated that only in uniting estranged worlds within one's self can external divisions be transcended in unity and peace. Proceeding on this conviction, Lao Tzu, Chuang Tzu and Jesus are placed "in dialogue" in the hopes that in being exposed to these touchpoints of mutual recognition, these grace notes of conceptual harmony, these passageways into the consciousness of the other, readers will be sensitized and prepared for a significant personal dialogical experience of their own—for the good of the entire human community.

道可道非常道
名可名非常名
無名天地之始
有名萬物之母
故常無欲以觀
其妙　常有　欲以
觀其妙　常有欲以觀其徼
此兩者同出而異名
同謂之玄　玄之又玄
眾妙之門

TO THE CHRISTIAN READER:
INTRODUCTION TO TAOISM.

It seems a realistic assumption that the majority of those who may pick up this book would be Christians who stand in need of familiarization with Taoism; the following outline is therefore provided as a short primer on Taoism to meet the assumed need.

FOUNDATIONAL TERMS.

TAOISM. Pronounced "Dow-ism." The term that encompasses both the theories that constitute Taoist philosophy *(Tao-chia)* and the magical ritualisms of Taoist religion *(Tao-chiao)*. (Note: As the two are completely separable in Chinese life and thought, this book concerns itself solely with the theoretical speculations of Taoist philosophy, to the total exclusion of Taoist folk-religious esoterica.) As a major component of Chinese religious sensibility, philosophical Taoism represents the intuitive, spontaneous, free and naturalistic pole that stands in dialectical opposition to the structured rationalism of Confucianism.[7]

TAO. Some words defy strict definition. Tao is one of them. As in all such cases, the best that can be done is to simply provide examples of the various ways the Tao is spoken of, and then hope that a correct conceptual orientation to the term is thereby inculcated:

"Tao is what there is...the fundamental metaphysical category...the 'real thing' or basic stuff as opposed to something merely phenomenal and synthetic.[8]

"Tao is equivalent of both the Greek word *logos,* or Word, and the Greek word *hodos,* the Way...the first principle—indeterminate, and yet that from which all things proceed to become determinate."[9]

"It is the all-encompassing first and last principle, the ground of all worlds before all worlds...indefinable, inexpressible, and indescribable."[10]

"Though the Tao is defined as 'the way,' it is most often compared to a stream or a moving body of water as it progresses endlessly and inexorably....For this reason it behooved mankind not to struggle against the Tao but to seek to blend with it and be guided by it."[11]

"The unchanging Being behind all reality....Also understood as the 'divine' pattern for humans to follow....Being as understood as Being in Becoming."[12]

"The way that gives all ways, the very source of our power to think what reason, mind, meaning, logos properly mean to say—properly, by their own nature."[13]

Presuming that a "feel" for the concept of the Tao has been successfully conveyed, one may now read authentic Taoist source material with a degree of understanding and appreciation of the subject matter. The *Tao Te Ching* speaks of Tao thusly:

"As Being [Tao] is named the mother of the Ten Thousand Things.
Thus, always in terms of No-thingness,
One contemplates its [hidden] wonders;
Always in terms of Being,
One contemplates its [manifest] forms.
These two spring forth from the same [source],
And yet they differ in name.
Both are called 'profoundly dark';
Profoundly dark and ever profoundly dark,
The gateway to infinite wonders." (Chapter 1)[14]

And again:

"The great Tao flows everywhere
It may go left or right.
The Ten Thousand Things derive their life from it,
and it never refuses them;
It accomplishes its task without claiming any name;
It restores and nourishes the Ten Thousand Things,

Without claiming any authority over them;
It remains desire-less;
It may be named 'the small':
The Ten Thousand Things return to it,
Yet it does not claim any authority over them;
It may be named 'the great';
Because it never claims greatness,
Therefore it can attain greatness." (Chapter 34)

FOUNDING FATHERS.

LAO TZU. A legendary sage who supposedly had the title Lao Tzu (the "Old Master") bestowed upon him by admiring and appreciative disciples. Ancient tradition relates that he was born in the state of Ch'u in 604 B.C. (Some modern scholars compute the date to 570 B.C., thus approximating him closer to the great Confucius; other scholars deny the reality of his existence entirely.) According to the received story of old, Lao Tzu held the prestigious position of curator of the imperial archives in the capital city of Loyang. After tiring of the artificialities of court life he migrated westward, but a guard refused permission to pass beyond the border of China until the old master committed to writing the sum of his wisdom. After producing the work known as the *Tao Te Ching,* Lao Tzu exited China, never to be heard from again.

CHUANG TZU. A philosopher (third century B.C.) who stands in relation to Lao Tzu as Mencius does to Confucius, that is, as a creative interpreter and popularizer of the original master.

SIGNIFICANT CONCEPTS.

CH'I. Literally "breath," but in the Taoist context the term carries the meaning of vital energy or life force. A noble goal in life is to remove the obstacles that prohibit the flow of ch'i. (The exercise program "t'ai-chi-chuan" that has won much popular acceptance in the Western world is in essence the applied technique of inviting ch'i from the cosmos to enter the practitioner's body in an unobstructed fashion; Chinese medicine and acupuncture apply this theoretical construct as well.)

P'U. The Uncarved Block. The master symbol for Tao and life in Tao-harmony characterized by such qualities as humility and simplicity, a lack of artifice, satisfaction with what one has been given in life, a pacifistic mindset, contentment with one's self, and a benevolent regard for all.

TE. Power or virtue in the sense of moral force or power; the way in which the universal Tao becomes particularized in the generation, unfolding and preservation of the world; the power of the naturalness, simplicity and integrity of creation.

T'IEN and *DI.* "Heaven" and "earth," often expressed in conjunction. Taken together, the pair stand for nature, or what is natural, having the function of covering and supporting, respectively. In some instances in the *Tao Te Ching,* heaven—again as a code word for nature without any supernatural connotation—is personalized and endowed with godlike attributes.

WU-WEI. Literally, "nonaction," in the sense of action without artificiality, aggressiveness, overaction or attachment; a disposition that should accompany contemplation of the universe such as to lead one to awareness of the Tao. It is to be kept in mind that when Taoism recommends such virtues as "nonaction," "nonknowledge," "nonstriving," "nonself," and the like, the use of the qualifier "non" does not carry the notion of negation, but rather serves as an invitation to contemplate the qualified term from the perspective of Tao.[15]

YIN and *YANG.* These terms are commonly misinterpreted as opposing elements of duality in creation (e.g., lightness and darkness, maleness and femaleness, heaven and earth, etc.); more correctly, they are to be understood as the complimentary aspects of the one Tao that exists before all opposites.

CLASSIC TEXTS.

TAO TE CHING. Literally, *The Classics of the Way and Its Power of Virtue.* A relatively short text, ascribed to Lao Tzu, it consists of eighty-one poems totalling about 5,200 words. The work is acknowledged to be second only to the *Analects of Confucius* in influence within the Chinese literary tradition, and second to the Christian Bible in number of world-wide publications. The main concerns of the *Tao Te Ching* are (1) to elucidate just how individuals and societies should order their existence in a way that is in tune with the flow of Tao, and (2) to instruct rulers in particular regarding proper attitudes and conduct that are consonant with such existence.

CHUANG TZU. The work bearing the name of the author and school to which the content is attributed. In the form of thirty-three essays totaling about one hundred thousand words, this collection is recognized as being brilliantly written; many witty anecdotes, entertaining allegories, and imaginary conversations enhance its literary charm.[16]

HUA HU CHING. A lesser known work of eighty-one short compositions that constitute the purported oral teachings of Lao Tzu that sought to relate the individual, rather than society as a whole, to Tao.

CONCLUDING STATEMENT.

Regarding the seminal point of resonance between Western-world Christian theology and Oriental cosmological thinking, Hans Küng has provided a cogent statement that is presented here as the conclusion to this subsection:

"What must be kept in mind is that, for both Taoist and Christian thought, the *innermost essence of the Tao, like that of God,* remains *hidden* to human beings. Whoever thinks he or she can sneak inside the mystery of God to get a kind of inside view of god suffers from the greatest self-delusion. Whoever thinks he or she has comprehended God has already misapprehended him. Whoever thinks he or she had

God in hand has come up empty-handed! His or her grasp extends literally into nothingness. On the basis of mystical theology and negative theology, Christians can therefore also understand completely why Taoists refuse all definitions, all naming of the Tao, whether positive or negative. Even Thomas Aquinas asserts that God's proper essence remains inaccessible to human reason and affirms what the mystic Pseudo-Dionysius says: '...wherefore man reaches the highest point of his knowledge about God when he knows that he knows him not, inasmuch as he knows that which is God transcends whatever he conceives of him....'In sum, even if Taoist (and mystical) thought can never be regulative for Christian theology, it must in any case act as definite corrective."[17]

TO THE CHRISTIAN READER:
PRINCIPLES OF DIALOGUE.

Can God's activity in the world through the Spirit be discerned apart from the particular revelation of Jesus Christ? Is an explicit "yes" to Christ necessary for salvation to be realized? Is God's work in people of other religious and philosophical traditions a preparation for receiving the gospel or is it complete in and of itself? Although these and similar questions touching upon the issue of salvation for non-Christians possess an interest of their own and are vigorously debated within the household of Christianity, the issue itself lies outside the purview of this work. With regard to the writing of this book, the opening and admonition provided by the remarks of James Fredericks obtained: "The comparative theologian seeks to place Christian discourse in conversation with discourses taken from various religions in the hope that they might enhance one another....To do Christian theology in such a manner does place Christian self-understanding at risk. To fail to do so would be to lose an opportunity for the enrichment of faith."[18] The authors of this book then proceeded in accordance with the following presumptions [19]:

A) The goals of interreligious dialogue, taken in its broadest sense, are the attainment of ever greater degrees of mutual understanding, respectful interaction in daily life, and shared service to the human community.

B) Faithfulness to God's plan for the world leads to meeting, hearing, knowing and communicating with persons and groups of other religious and philosophical traditions; Christians, along with others, need to learn about those different from themselves at all levels of society and strive to live as neighbors, not strangers.

C) Christians bear witness as a response to the good news of Christ through word and deed, through proclamation of acts of love and justice; inherent in being loving and just is knowing and respecting others.

D) Encounters with non-Christian persons or thought systems do not require a lessening of commitment to one's own understanding of the revelation of God through Jesus Christ; personal conviction need not be compromised or relativized.

E) The study of a religious or philosophical tradition different from one's own can deepen one's understanding of God, clarify one's faith perspective, and enhance one's spirituality.

NOTES ON THE TRANSLATIONS.

The authors of this book are proud to place into print the previously unpublished translation of the *Tao Te Ching* produced by the combined efforts of Dr. Charles Wei-Hsun Fu and Dr. Sandra A. Wawrytko. Dr. Fu (d. 14 October 1996) taught in the Religion Department of Temple University for twenty-five years. He previously had taught at the Ohio State University and National Taiwan University, and was one of the founding faculty of Fo Kuang University in Taiwan. He was the editor of nine series of Chinese and English language books, ranging from Asian thought and culture to modern Buddhism, life-and-death studies, and current global trends. Dr. Wawrytko has taught at San Diego State University since 1980 in both the department of philosophy and the Asian studies program. Previously she taught at Washington University and the Chinese Culture University in Taiwan. Dr. Wawrytko is also founder and executive director of the International Society for Philosophy and Psychotherapy, and is an editor of a series in that same field for SUNY Press.

The *New American Bible* (*Catholic Study Bible* Edition, Oxford University Press, 1990) is the source of the biblical citations. This translation is a product of the rigorous Catholic biblical scholarship—aided by Protestant expertise—that was summoned by the Second Vatican Council.

Burton Watson's *The Complete Works of Chuang Tzu* (Columbia University Press, 1968) is a work of irreproachable scholarship that possesses the added grace of being written in a style that enhances the *Chuang Tzu's* accessibility to a general readership; it has maintained for itself the reputation for being the standard to which all other translations of the *Chuang Tzu* are compared.

Brian Walker's translation of the *Hua Hu Ching* (Clark City Press, 1992) has been praised as a valuable contribution to the body of Taoist literature in English.

NOTES ON PRIME RESOURCES
FOR THE THEMATIC COMMENTARIES.

Extensive treatments of each theme within each tradition would constitute small libraries in themselves. In the alternative, it is intended that
the provision of carefully considered representative voices will, in the
cumulative effect, suffice in conveying to the reader what it is to look
out upon the world, and within one's self, from Christian and Taoist
viewpoints.

The Christian commentators are predominantly from the Catholic
tradition, though a conscious effort was made to include references to
individuals and resource works from other Christian traditions as well.

Philokalia is Greek for "love for what is beautiful (or good)," and
names an anthology that addresses aspects of ascetic and mystical
theology that constitute a primary sourcebook for the spiritual tradition
of Eastern Orthodoxy. Originally published in 1782 by St. Macarius of
Corinth (1731–1805) and St. Nicodemus of the Holy Mountain
(1749–1809), this anthology comprises many of the complete works of
over thirty different authors extending from the fourth to the fifteenth
centuries.

The lucidity of thought, clarity of expression, and soundness of scholarship exhibited by Ellen M. Chen's *The Tao Te Ching: A New Translation
with Commentary* (Paragon House, 1989) are of such quality that, if a
single book introducing the thought and spirit of Taoism were required,
this would be a worthy recommendation.

Lao-Tzu's Taoteching (Mercury House, 1996) by Red Pine (born
William Porter) provides valuable commentaries on the work of Lao Tzu
that were produced through the past two millenniums.

Michael LaFargue's *The Tao of the Tao Te Ching: A Translation and
Commentary* (State University of New York Press, 1992) is distinguished by its helpful topical glossary and paraphrasing of Lao Tzu's
teachings in modern language.

Wing-Tsit Chan, in serving as a reference for Drs. Fu and Wawrytko,
qualifies as an "authority for the authorities"; quotations from his *The
Way of the Tao* (Bobbs-Merrill, 1963) are extracted with confidence.

ABBREVIATIONS AND TEXTUAL NOTES.

TTC = *Tao Te Ching;* translation and notations are the work of Dr. Charles Wei-Hsun Fu and Dr. Sandra A. Wawrytko. The bracketed inter-polations are as they appear in their manuscript.

HHC = *Hua Hu Ching;* copied from the translation done by Brian Walker and published under that title by Clark City Press (Livingston, Montana: 1992).

All scriptural quotations are taken from *The Catholic Study Bible,* Donald Senior, general editor (New York: Oxford University Press, 1990).

All quotations of Chuang Tzu are from Burton Watson's *The Complete Works of Chuang Tzu* (New York: Columbia University Press, 1968).

ABUNDANCE.

Lao Tzu: "Who can have excess to offer the world?
Only those who follow Tao." (TTC, 77)

Jesus: "'And do you not remember, when I broke the five loaves for the five thousand, how many wicker baskets full of fragments you picked up?' They answered him, 'Twelve.' 'When I broke the seven loaves for the four thousand, how many full baskets of fragments did you pick up?' They answered [him], 'Seven.' He said to them, 'Do you still not understand?'"
(Mk 8:18–21)

ABUNDANCE.

Thierry Maertens, O.S.B.: "Miracles of multiplication were numerous in the Bible. Though they might have aided the hungry, they were, however, often the sign of God's special salvation over His people, and still further, the sign of happiness promised in messianic abundance.

"In fact, when Christ undertook the multiplication of loaves it meant that the messianic era had arrived. But successive versions concentrated on giving these miracles a spiritual meaning, first by interpreting them as Eucharistic figures; later, especially with John, by giving them eternal dimensions: the bread that was multiplied was imperishable, giving access to everlasting life.

"Thereafter, the image of multiplication coincided with the theme of the abundance of graces."[1]

Peter K. H. Lee suggests Lao Tzu would have responded with a serene smile of delight if he were to be exposed to the various biblical images of vital, joyful, and energy-filled abundance. Those who seek to attune themselves to Tao-nature would experience, according to Lee, "an unfathomable depth which is like a deep well from which can be drawn refreshing water without end."[2]

ACCEPTANCE.

Chuang Tzu: "I received life because the time had come; I will lose it because the order of things passes on. Be content with this time and dwell in this order and then neither sorrow nor joy can touch you. In ancient times this was called 'freeing of the bound.' There are those who cannot free themselves, because they are bound by things. But nothing can ever win against Heaven—that's the way it's always been." (Chapter 6, "The Great and Venerable Teacher")

Lao Tzu: "When the people have no fear of death,
Then why threaten them with death?" (TTC, 74)

Jesus (to Judas): "What you are going to do, do quickly." (Jn 13:27)

ACCEPTANCE.

Spiritual director Anthony de Mello, S.J., suggested that, from the perspective of eternity, Jesus and Judas are to be seen in all victims and persecutors, the crucified and the killers; one melody in the contrasting notes, one dance moving through different steps.[1] Imputing to Jesus the eternal perspective, to acquiesce to the conditions leading to his death is but to "dance" the will of the one he called "Father."

After transposing the notion of acquiescence to Taoistic "being empty and resting in nonaction" and the "will of the Father" to the "is-ness" of creation, chapter 36 of the Xisheng jing ("Scripture of Western Ascension," a fifth-century Taoist text of unknown authorship) can be read as a recommendation of acceptance rooted in the awareness of *tzu jan* (it-is-what-it-is). Laozi says: "All beings have their place of return, whether they desire it or not. Emptiness returns to the Tao, spirit returns to the virtue. Clarity returns to heaven, turbidity to earth. Water returns to moisture, fire to heat. Without desiring to become visible as bodies, people yet become incarnate and can be seen. Without being required to do so, birds and beasts return to mountains and marshes, fish and dragons to the seas and rivers. When you can be empty and rest in nonaction, even if you never desire the Tao, it will return to you naturally."[2]

ACCOMPLISHMENT.

Lao Tzu: "The best [general] achieves the objective and stops,
But dares not seek to dominate the world,
Achieves the objective without bragging;
Achieves the objective without boasting;
Achieves the objective without arrogance...." (TTC, 30)

"Withdraw when your task is accomplished,
[This reflects] the Tao of Heaven."[a] (TTC, 9)

Jesus: "I glorified you [Father] on earth by accomplishing the work that you gave me to do....I have given them the glory you gave me, so that they may be one, as we are one, I in them and you in me, that they may be brought to perfection as one...." (Jn 17:4, 22–23)

"It is finished." (Jn 19:30)

---

[a]Here the translators note that in the context of Taoism, *t'ien* or *heaven* always must be understood as *nature* or what is natural (*tzu-jan*), in sharp contrast to the Confucian notion of *t'ien* as the *transcendent heaven.*

ACCOMPLISHMENT.

When contemporary readers consider John 17, they are given a glimpse of life with God that transcends conventional limits and expectations. This prayer points the faith community toward a future in which God's governance and care of them is complete, in which the experience of God's love for them is realized. The believer is enabled in daily life, because, as this prayer is a reminder, God is responsible for the nurture of the future. This eschatological vision, too, is not cause for facile triumphalism, because it is grounded in the inescapable reality of Jesus' hour of supreme sacrifice. Yet this prayer invites the faith community to believe, as Jesus believed at his hour, that "the love with which you have loved me may be in them, and I in them." (Jn 17:26).[1]

The sense of equilibrium that crowns achievement is a quality that is present at each moment throughout the achieving. Arthur Waley explicates: "The case is cited of a philosopher who possessed this 'poise' to such a degree that he could land a huge fish from a deep pool with a line consisting of a single filament of raw silk. A line snaps at the point where most strain is put upon it. But if, owing to the perfect equilibrium of the fisherman's hand, no such point exists, the slenderest thread can bear the greatest imaginable weight without breaking. The Taoists indeed saw in many arts and crafts the utilization of a power akin if not identical with that of the Tao. The wheelwright, the carpenter, the butcher, the bowman, the swimmer, achieve their skill not by accumulating facts concerning their art, nor by the energetic use either of muscles or outward senses; but through utilizing the fundamental kinship which, underneath apparent distinctions and diversities, unites their own Primal Stuff to the Primal Stuff of the medium in which they work."[2]

Ellen M. Chen: "The very idea of Tao as change means that Tao, always moving forward, never remains at one set point. Thus if Tao accomplishes all things, it lets go of all things. This does not mean that Tao abandons what it has accomplished to move on to new things....Tao 'acts without holding onto' means that Tao, being an ever living creativity, does not impede the self-development of the beings it has created. This is meant to contrast with the human tendency to hold on to what they have accomplished, refusing to let go, thus frustrating the inner dynamisms of the processes they have helped shape."[3]

ASCETICISM/MODERATION.

Lao Tzu: "The world is a sacred vessel
It may not be mishandled,
[Nor may it be coveted.]
Whoever mishandles it will ruin it.
Whoever covets it will lose it.
Therefore among things, some walk ahead, some follow behind;
Some blow hot, some blow cold;
Some are strong, some are weak;
Some are at peace, some are endangered.
Accordingly, the Sage discards extremes, extravagance, and excess."
(TTC, 29)

"While worldlings make merry,
As if enjoying sacrificial banquets,
As if climbing the terrace in spring;
I remain detached,
Like an infant who has yet to smile." (TTC, 20)

"Then Jesus was led by the Spirit into the desert to be tempted by the devil. He fasted for forty days and forty nights...." (Mt 4:1–2)

ASCETICISM/MODERATION.

Robert Taft, S.J.: "The New Testament says practically nothing about what is often understood today as penance: the infliction of self-punishment. New Testament penance is *metanoia:* the imitation of Jesus by putting off the old Adam to put on the new, dying to self so that we rise again in Christ. And this implies asceticism....This asceticism is nothing more than the necessary objectivity and distance from whatever is impermanent and secondary in the human endeavor; the self-discipline necessary to maintain true freedom and make the right choices, the destruction of egoism by the honest person who has the courage to stand naked before God....[The point of it all is] not turning in on self, not a concentration on self-discipline as some sort of spiritual athletics, but an openness to new life, and through it an openness to others, the end to which it is all supposed to lead."[1]

Thomas Ryan: "Men and women from Jesus to Augustine to Aquinas to Teresa of Avila to Martin Luther to John Calvin to John Henry Newman to Martin Luther King all discovered that abstaining from food freed them to focus upon God with fresh intensity and opened avenues of spiritual perception and understanding that were not available during the rush of routine living. They found that as they focused upon God by the deliberate discipline of fasting, that God focused upon them and spoke to their hearts with clarity of direction and quickening of spirit....

"Growth in spirituality is the slow work of God's grace helping us to fully accept and harmoniously integrate all the dimensions of our selves. When bodiliness and spiritedness become in my consciousness but two dimensions of my one being, I am on the way to holiness, which is wholeness."[2]

To live the Way, to "hold to the Uncarved Block," is to live in the pure simplicity and naturalness of Tao, without over- indulgence, ostentation or excess. In Taoism, asceticism is not a virtue to be intentionally cultivated, but the estimation by those who do not live the Tao of those who do.

"Li Hsi-Chai [fl. 1167] says, 'The sage considers his body transitory and the world its temporary lodging. How can he rule what is not his and lose the true and lasting Way?'"[3]

AWARENESS.

Lao Tzu: "Those who are highly evolved maintain an undiscriminating perception.
Seeing everything, labeling nothing, they maintain
their awareness of the Great Oneness.
Thus they are supported by it." (HHC, 19)

"It is always present and always available.
When speech is exhausted and mind dissolved, it
presents itself.
When clarity and purity are cultivated, it reveals itself.
If you are willing to be lived by it, you will see it everywhere, even in the most ordinary things." (HHC, 22)

Jesus: "But blessed are your eyes, because they see, and your ears, because they hear. Amen, I say to you, many prophets and righteous people longed to see what you see but did not see it, and to hear what you hear but did not hear it." (Mt 13:16–17)

AWARENESS.

To truly see and hear is to truly comprehend. Mother Julian of Norwich (four-teenth century) can be considered exemplary in the realm of religious aware-ness: "He shewed me a little thing the size of a hazelnut, lying in the palm of my hand; and it was as round as a ball. I looked thereupon with the eye of my understanding, and thought: What may this be? And it was answered generally thus: It is all that is made. I marvelled how it could last, for it seemed so little it might suddenly have fallen to naught. And I was answered in my understand-ing: It lasteth, and ever shall, because God loveth it. And so the world hath its existence by the love of God."[1]

Agnes C. J. Lee: "The whole New Testament teaches that it is through faith that Christ's followers enter into the salvation of resurrection. However, in Christian teaching there has been a strong tendency to present faith merely as a mental assent to dogma. Existentially, faith is nothing but an act of seeing, a vision into the true nature of oneself, others, the world, and reality. Inasmuch as this is not yet full seeing, we call it 'faith.' As this faith-seeing grows, one comes to what Zen Buddhists call 'seeing one's true nature'....Jesus, in his risen state, is calling humans to this type of seeing. He is a true seer who sees people, things and the world as they are. Faith is the Christian's sharing in Christ's self-identification and his vision of reality."[2]

Lee writes of Chuang Tzu: "[He] conveys to us that when we *see* things, events, even life-death in the light of Tao, in other words, through personal existential experience of the ultimate, then nothing is better, nothing is worse, nothing is important and nothing is unimportant. There is only unceasingly transforming Life itself. This is the true nature of all things and the real face before we were born. When we see this reality, we are one with the Great Ultimate (God) and we are the True Man, Real Man and God Man."[3]

CHILDLIKENESS.

Lao Tzu: "One whose virtue is deep can be compared to an infant." (TTC, 55)

"Can you control your vital force (Ch'i),[a]
To attain the suppleness like an infant?" (TTC, 10)

"Whoever becomes the ravine of the world,
Without departing from the eternal virtue,
Will return to infancy." (TTC, 28)

Jesus: "Amen, I say to you, unless you turn and become like children, you will not enter the kingdom of heaven. Whoever humbles himself like this child is the greatest in the kingdom of heaven. And whoever receives one child such as this in my name receives me." (Mt 18:3–5)

"Let the children come to me, and do not prevent them; for the kingdom of heaven belongs to such as these." (Mt 19:14)

---

[a]The Chinese character *'ch'i'* means 'vital force' in general, or 'cosmic energy' existent prior to the polarization of matter and spirit. According to ancient Chinese cosmology, the unity of Heaven and humanity is predicated on the macrocosmic/microcosmic sharing of *ch'i*. Often this is understood in terms of the primordial forces of *yin* (associated with Earth, the receptive or feminine principle, etc.) and *yang* (associated with Heaven, the creative or masculine principle, etc.).—Translators.

CHILDLIKENESS.

Walter Burghardt poses, and answers, the question, "What childlike qualities should characterize candidates for the kingdom?" Children are refreshingly fresh, not faded or jaded by the years. They are open rather than cynical, delighted to be surprised. They are rarely if ever suspicious. And, most pertinent, little ones can only receive, can only respond spontaneously to love and affection. They have no claim to achievement, nothing they can proudly claim as their own. To enter the kingdom is to accept the dominion of Jesus, not to lapse into second childhood or to reproduce the baby and the adolescent. It is to recapture—in an adult fashion and in the face of God—the openness and nakedness, the sheer receptivity and utter dependence; such is what Jesus wants to see in his disciples.[1]

St. Francis de Sales advised: "...behave as little children do, who with one hand cling to their father, and with the other gather strawberries or blackberries along the hedges...."[2]

Ellen M. Chen: "The infant, not knowing the union of male and female, holds to the 'One,' which is the womb of the universe. Breathing softly and possessing the power of life in the fullest degree, the infant is harmed by nothing. To breath softly like the infant is called womb-breathing....If Freud shows life from infancy on to be one of struggle, conflict and neuroses, the Taoist retreat to infancy and the womb is the way back to the peace and bliss in the universal ocean of life....Han-shan Te-ch'ing (1546–1623) comments:

'The infant neither knows nor recognizes anything. Its life force being full it exists in forgetfulness (*wang*). One who forgets things is also forgotten by things. Thus it mingles with the animals without disturbing their groupings; it mingles with birds without disturbing their flights. Even ferocious creatures do not harm it, as it does not have a vulnerable spot. Such is the fullness of its life force....'

"The infant enjoys this special blessing because it is both internally and externally unified. Its internal unity is due to the perfection of its life force (*ching*); its external unity is due to the perfection of its harmony (*ho*) with all. To begin with the infant's bones are soft and its sinews tender. Since the soft and tender belong to life while the hard and strong head toward death (chapter 76 of the *Tao Te Ching*), the infant has a firm grip on life....

"That the infant can cry all day without getting hoarse shows that whatever it does it does without ill effects. Its crying is neither the expression of a Nietzschean will to power aimed at overcoming others, nor what Sartre calls an act of bad faith veiling its own impotence while putting others in the wrong. The infant is not intentional. Its crying is spontaneous, like a tempest full of sound and fury while raging but, once subsided, restoring the earth to calm (chapter 23). The infant may cry all day but it is in harmony (*ho*) with all."[3]

DARKNESS.

Lao Tzu: "Profoundly dark and ever profoundly dark, the gateway to infinite wonders."[a] (TTC, 1)

Jesus: "My God, my God, why have you forsaken me?" (Mk 15:34)

---

[a] The Chinese character *'hsuan'* originally depicted a piece of silk thread which had been dipped in dye, and thus darkened. Hence, it means 'dark,' and by extension became 'deep,' 'profound,' 'wondrous,' or 'mysterious.'—Translators.

DARKNESS.

In speaking the opening line of Psalm 22 while in the throes of death upon the cross, Jesus expresses profound identification with lost Israel. Christian spiritual masters through the centuries have written of a sense of complete and final abandonment as the necessary prelude to divine union, John of the Cross being foremost among them. John wrote of the state of feeling alone, stripped of any remaining spiritual gratification or comprehendible consoling image, and disabused of any notion of self-reliance or initiative as the "dark night of the soul":

"We may say that there are three reasons for which this journey made by the soul to union with God is called night. The first has to do with the point from which the soul goes forth, for it has gradually to deprive itself of desire for all the worldly things which it possessed by denying them to itself; the which denial and deprivation are as it were night to all the senses of man. The second reason has to do with the mean or road along which the soul must travel to this union—that is faith, which is likewise as dark as night to the understanding. The third has to do with the point to which it travels, namely God, who equally is dark night of the soul in this life. These three nights must pass through the soul—or rather the soul must pass through them—in order that it may come to divine union with God."[1]

William Johnston notes the possiblity that Jesus had the whole of the psalm in mind as he was dying. This is significant in light of the fact that the psalm is of the messianic type, ending as it does with a vision of all peoples from the ends of the earth turning to the Lord in remembrance, joy, hope and worship. This is a cry of resurrection, the realization that in the total loss there is the total gain. In the nothingness there is the everything, in death there is the victory.[2]

Peter K. H. Lee points out that, in the workings of Tao, it is precisely in helplessness that the power of rejuvenation and fulfillment becomes most present and effective.[3]

DISINTERESTED VIRTUE.

Lao Tzu: "Supreme virtue is nonvirtuous,
Therefore it has virtue;
Inferior virtue does not lose its virtue,
Therefore it has not virtue." (TTC, 38)

"To practice virtue is to selflessly offer assistance to others,
giving without limitation one's time,
abilities, and possessions in service,
whenever and wherever needed,
without prejudice concerning the identity of those in need.
If your willingness to give blessings is limited,
so also is your ability to receive them.
This is the subtle operation of the Tao. (HHC, 4)

Jesus: "When the Son of Man comes in his glory, and all the angels with him, he will sit upon his glorious throne, and all the nations will be assembled before him. And he will separate them one from another, as a shepherd separates the sheep from the goats. He will place the sheep on his right and the goats on his left. Then the king will say to those on his right, 'Come, you who are blessed by my Father. Inherit the kingdom prepared for you from the foundation of the world. For I was hungry and you gave me food, I was thirsty and you gave me drink, a stranger and you welcomed me, naked and you clothed me, ill and you cared for me, in prison and you visited me.' Then the righteous will answer him and say, 'Lord, when did we see you hungry and feed you, or thirsty and give you drink? When did we see you a stranger and welcome you, or naked and clothe you? When did we see you ill or in prison, and visit you?' And the king will say to them in reply: 'Amen, I say to you, whatever you did for one of these least brothers of mine, you did for me.' Then he will say to those on his left, 'Depart from me, you accursed, into the eternal fire prepared for the devil and his angels....'" (Mt 25: 31–41)

DISINTERESTED VIRTUE.

Orthodox Archbishop Anthony Bloom speaks of this parable, not so much in its usual interpretation as a statement of death, judgment and hopeless finality, but as a story about living: "...neither the sinners nor the just are asked anything by God about their convictions or their ritual observances; all the Lord appraises is the degree to which they have been human." The Archbishop continues: "Being human requires, however, imagination, a sense of humour and of occasion, and a realistic and loving concern for the true needs and wishes of the object—or shall we say the victim—of our care. Here is a story from the lives of the Desert Fathers to illustrate the point. After a full, brilliant social and political life at the court of Byzantium, St. Arsenius retired into the desert of Egypt, seeking for complete solitude and contemplative silence. A lady of the court, who had been a great admirer of his, sought him out in the wilderness. She fell at his feet. 'Father,' she exclaimed, 'I have undertaken this perilous journey to see you and hear from you just one commandment which I vow to keep all my life!' 'If you truly pledge yourself never to disobey my will, here is my commandment: If you ever hear that I am in one place, go to another!' Is not this what many would say to all those do-gooders whose virtue they are doomed to endure? To me, the point of the parable of the sheep and the goats is this: if you have been truly and wisely human, you are ready to enter into the divine realm, to share what is God's own, as Eternal Life is nothing else than God's own life shared by him with his creatures...we shall be capable of living the life of Heaven, partaking of the nature of God, filled with his Spirit."[1]

"Yen Tsun [fl. 53–24 B.C.] says, 'The person who embodies the Way is empty and effortless, yet he leads all creatures to the Way. The person who embodies virtue is faultless and responsive and ready to do anything. The person who embodies kindness shows love for all creatures without restriction. The person who embodies justice deals with things by matching name with reality. The person who embodies ritual is humble and reveres harmony. These five are footprints of the Tao. They are not the ultimate goal. The ultimate goal is not one, much less five.'"[2]

EMPTY WORDS.

Lao Tzu: "Whoever knows does not speak;
Whoever speaks does not know." (TTC, 56)

"Nature says little." (TTC, 23)

"Excessive words tend toward self-exhaustion." (TTC, 5)

"With all this talking, what has been said?
The subtle truth can be pointed at with words,
but it can't be contained by them." (HHC, 81)

Chuang Tzu: "The fish trap exists because of the fish; once you've gotten
the fish, you can forget the trap. The rabbit snare exists because of the
rabbit; once you've gotten the rabbit, you can forget the snare. Words
exists because of meaning; once you've gotten the meaning, you can
forget the words. Where can I find a man who has forgotten words so I
can have a word with him?" (Chapter 26, "External Things")

*Jesus: "Not everyone who says to me, 'Lord, Lord,' will enter the kingdom
of heaven, but only the one who does the will of my Father in heaven."
(Mt 7:21)*

*"Again Pilate questioned him, 'Have you no answer? See how many
things they accuse you of.' Jesus gave him no further answer, so that
Pilate was amazed." (Mk 15:4–5)*

EMPTY WORDS.

Frederick Buechner reminds that the Hebrew term *dabar* means both "word" and "deed." To say something with sincerity is to do something. For God, having spoken light is having created light. For us mere mortals, loving, hating or forgiving is effected in addressing the other when there was but ambiguous silence prior to the saying.[1] In relation to the one believed by Christians to be the "Word of God" (Jn 1:1), merely mouthing the syllable of belief—"Lord"—without belief is to refuse the power of the word (Word). From the perspective of the spiritual master, if the conditions are such that a word cannot be incarnated into action, it would be better to keep silent: "Some brothers...went to see Abba Felix and they begged him to say a word to them. But the old man kept silence. After they had asked for a long time he said to them, 'You wish to hear a word?' They said, 'Yes, abba.' Then the old man said to them, 'There are not more words nowadays. When the brothers used to consult old men and when they did what was said to them, God showed them how to speak. But now, since they ask without doing that which they hear, God has withdrawn the grace of the word from the old men and they do not find anything to say, since there are no longer any who carry their words out.' Hearing this, the brothers groaned, saying, 'Pray for us, abba.'"[2]

St. Isaac of Syria, "Directions on Spiritual Training," from the *Philokalia:* "Not only does the guarding of the tongue speed the mind towards God, but it also give great hidden strength for performing external actions with the help of the body, and enlightens a man in the secret doing, as the fathers said; for guarding of the lips makes the conscience rise towards God, if only a man keeps silence with understanding."[3]

For Lao Tzu, the uncreated Tao, being uncreated and supremely wordless in itself, is of course uncircumscribable by words—as love, hate and forgiveness are uncircumscribable in relation to their creating words.

FLORA IMAGERY.

Lao Tzu: "All things flourish,
Each returning to its own root [Tao].
Returning to the root is called 'tranquility';
This is called 'returning to [natural] destiny';
'Returning to destiny' is called 'the eternal' [Tao].
To know the eternal is called 'enlightenment.'"[a] (TTC, 16)

"Grass and trees are supple and resilient when alive;[b]
Dry and withered when dead.
Thus the hard and stiff is the companion of death;
The supple and tender the companion of life." (TTC, 76)

Jesus: "This is how it is with the kingdom of God; it is as if a man were to scatter seed on the land and would sleep and rise night and day and the seed would sprout and grow, he knows not how. Of its own accord the land yields fruit, first the blade, then the ear, then the full grain in the ear. And when the grain is ripe, he wields the sickle at once, for the harvest has come." (Mk 4:26–29)

"The kingdom of heaven is like a mustard seed that a person took and sowed in a field. It is the smallest of all the seeds, yet when full-grown it is the largest of plants. It becomes a large bush, and the 'birds of the sky come and dwell in its branches.'" (Mt 13:31–32)

---

[a] It is interesting to note that the original character for 'enlightenment' is '*ming,*' a composite of the characters for sun (*jih*) and moon (*yueh*). Hence, we have translated the word as 'enlightenment' rather than 'clarity,' in that the latter represents the literal meaning but one which is hermeneutically unsupported by the context.—Translators.

[b] In some editions, this line includes the phrase 'the Ten Thousand Things' prior to the mention of grass and trees, which is probably a later interpolation.—Translators.

FLORA IMAGERY.

To the question, "What one term best summarizes all that Jesus preached, prayed for, lived for, died and arose for?" responses usually include the words "love," "life," "forgiveness," "truth," "peace," and "justice." According to the gospel tradition itself, the correct term that recapitulates all other terms is "kingdom," best construed as the exercise of God's sovereignty in which all the above suggested concepts—all that we would wish for ourselves and our loved ones to infinite degree—find their ultimate and eternal realization. To illustrate how the kingdom could be considered at once as a fact that is present, and at the same time a reality whose full revelation is still to come, Jesus employed an image from nature: just as a tree is "latent" within its seed at its planting, so is the fullness of the kingdom in relation to his coming. Wilfred J. Harrington, O.P., notes: "The little seed of the kingdom has within it, implanted there by God, its own principle of growth, an intimate and irresistible force, which will bring it to fulfillment."[1]

St. Paul, commenting on the role of God's ministers: "What is Apollos, after all, and what is Paul? Ministers through whom you became believers, just as the Lord assigned each one. I planted, Apollos watered, but God caused the growth. Therefore, neither the one who plants nor the one who waters is anything, but only God, who causes the growth. The one who plants and the one who waters are equal, and each will receive wages in proportion to his labor. For we are God's co-workers; you are God's field...." (1 Cor 3:5–9).

E. M. Chen: "Just as a living plant is tender and yielding, so is Tao weak and yielding. With plants the hidden roots support the visible leaves and flowers, which return to the roots upon perishing. Likewise, Tao is the hidden root, the nonbeing from which all beings spring and to which all beings return. The life of a plant is conditioned by seasonal rotation. So is the movement of Tao in four stages: great (summer), disappearing (fall), far away (winter), and return (spring). In the same way does the Taoist model spiritual life after a plant. A living plant is tender and pliant, while a dead plant is stiff and hard; one who is with Tao is also tender and pliant, while one who departs from Tao is stiff and hard. The plant kingdom is a quiet kingdom that sleeps in beauty; Taoist quietude is the spiritual condition of regeneration..."[2]

Liu I–Ming (eighteenth century): "Plants and trees first flower and then produce fruit, each in its season. This is why they can live a long time. If they miss their season, this is a foresign of death, because it is abnormal.

"What I realize as I observe this is the Tao of going along with time.

"What human life depends on is spirit and energy. When events take place people cannot but respond to them, and when things come up they cannot but deal with them. Using events to control events, organizing things according to what is there, not looking forward to what has not come, not dwelling on what has passed, the spirit is not injured and the energy is not dissipated. This is like plants and trees flowering and fruiting in season; this is the enlivening path.

"If people are greedy and passionate, ambitious and always conniving, forming strategies for events that are yet to come, clinging to events that have already passed, the spirit and energy become worn out. This is like plants and trees flowering and blooming out of season; this is the road to death."[3]

THE GREAT UNKNOWABLE/UNNAMEABLE.

Lao Tzu: "The Tao[a] that can be taoed[b] is not the eternal Tao;
The name that can be named is not the eternal name." (TTC, 1)

"Unseeable, ungraspable, the Tao is beyond any
attempt to analyze or categorize it.
At the same time, its truth is everywhere you turn.
If you can let go of it with your mind and surround it
with your heart, it will live inside you forever." (HHC, 33)

"If you go searching for the Great Creator, you will
come back empty-handed.
The source of the universe is ultimately unknowable,
a great invisible river flowing forever
through a vast and fertile valley.
Silent and uncreated, it creates all things." (HHC, 39)

Jesus: "You do not know [the Father]....But I do know him and I keep his word." (Jn 8:55)

---

[a] The word 'Tao' literally means 'the Way,' 'road,' or 'path.' Since Tao has become incorporated into the English language, it remains untranslated throughout the text, in order to convey the essential flavor of Taoism.—Translators.
[b] Due to the grammatical flexibility of the Chinese language, the word 'tao' can function as noun, verb or modifier. Here it is used as a verb and has the meaning 'to follow,' 'to express,' or 'to speak of.'—Translators.

THE GREAT UNKNOWABLE/UNNAMEABLE.

The principle of the unknowability of the divine essence by the created intellect has one of its classic expressions in the writing of the influential sixth-century theologian known as Pseudo-Dionysius: "[God] is described as invisible, infinite, ungraspable, and other things which show not what He is but what in fact He is not. This second way of talking about Him seems to me much more appropriate, for, as the secret of sacred tradition has instructed, God is in no way like the things that have being and we have no knowledge at all of His incomprehensible and ineffable transcendence and invisibility."[1] This "apophatic" or "negative" type of theologizing represents a major tradition in Christian thought.

For Lao Tzu, to name is to introduce that which is named into the realm of the comprehensible, the graspable, the finite, and the individuated; trying to name the unknowable Tao in the attempt to grasp it by the knowing mind would be an attempt on Tao's original unity and simplicity. Wing-Tsit Chan notes that with regard to naming, Taoism distinguishes itself from Confucianism, Legalism, and the School of Logicians, who regard names as necessary for human progress and social organization. It should be noted however, that Taoism has not gone as far as Buddhism, which rejects naming and characterization as falsifying reality.[2]

GROUND OF BEING.

Lao Tzu: " Tao gives life to [the Ten Thousand Things];
Its virtue fosters them;
Matter[a] shapes their forms;
[Natural] forces perfect them.
Accordingly, the Ten Thousand Things cannot but honor Tao,
and exalt its virtue.
They receive no mandate [of Heaven][b]
To honor Tao and exalt its virtue.
Thus, Tao gives life to them...." (TTC, 51)

"To integrate the positive influences, consciously reconnect yourself with
the primary energy ray of the Subtle Origin by adopting the practices of
the Integral Way." (HHC, 57)

*Jesus: "I am the true vine, and my Father is the vine grower...you are the
branches." (Jn 15:1–5)*

---

[a] 'Matter' ('*wu*,' literally 'things') signifies the primordial (cosmic) vital force (*ch'i*)
of the Ten Thousand Things.—Translators.

[b] The reason why we add 'of Heaven' is to make explicit the implied reference
to the Mandate of Heaven (*t'ien-ming*), a concept which, although advocated
by Confucianism, is inherently unacceptable to the Taoist.—Translators.

GROUND OF BEING.

In the scriptures, St. Paul addresses the Athenians: "What therefore you unknowingly worship, I proclaim to you. The God who made the world and all that is in it, the Lord of heaven and earth, does not dwell in sanctuaries made by human hands, nor is he served by human hands because he needs anything. Rather it is he who gives everyone life and breath and everything....'In him we live and move and have our being,' as even some of your poets have said, 'For we too are his offspring.'" (Acts 17:23–28)

Theologically speaking, Anglican theologian John Macquarrie reminds us that "God" and "being" are not synonyms. Rather, God is held to be the ever present, manifest, incomparable, active, enabling, empowering and personal principle that *lets-be*. As letting-be is more primordial than being, God is for each created "I" addressable as the uncreated, mysterious, transcendent, and wholly other "Thou."[1] In Jesus' intimate prayer to the Father on the eve of his death (chapter 17 of John), Jesus presents himself as glorifier and the glorified in relation to his Father.

In Christianity, that which lets be is the ground of the creation that is. In Taoism, the fundamental dichotomy is not between being and letting-be, but being and nonbeing, the latter pair issuing from the even more primordial Tao. E. M. Chen writes of the relation between Tao and the world:

"The relationship between Tao and the world in Taoism is much more intimate than the relationship between God and the world in Christianity. In Christianity the Son was begotten, not made, hence the intimate relationship between the Father and the Son who are indeed of the same substance (consubstantiation). The world was made, not begotten: God and the world do not share the same substance. The Taoist world, however, is indeed begotten by Tao: Tao gives birth to the world as a mother gives birth to her child. Still the Taoist world does not have the same substance as Tao. Tao as mother has no substance, it is nothing (wu)...The mother alone is everlasting."[2] Unfortunately, Chen did not take into account the Christian belief in the incarnation (the Son becoming consubstantial with humanity) in her assessment of relative degrees of "intimacy."

The Taoist sage does not acknowledge a transcendent creator God, but as Mary Carman Rose points out, neither is he or she wistful nor indifferent to the ground of Tao as the mystery beyond all mysteries; she suggests seeing Taoism as a pre-Christian glimpse of what comes to be revealed as the divine creativity which includes the beneficent appropriation of all human activities.[3]

"INJUSTICE" RESOLVED.

Lao Tzu: "If I have a little knowledge [of Tao],
And walk on the great Way [Tao],
I only fear going astray [into evil].
The great Tao is very even,
And yet people[a] love the bypaths.
Then the court is lavishly appointed,[b]
Weeds flourish in the field,
And the granaries are emptied.
Yet there are those sumptuously dressed,
Carrying well-honed swords,
Gluttonous in food and drink,
Possessed of riches and goods in excess.
This is called 'robbery [motivated by] extravagance.'
What a violation of Tao!" (TTC, 53)

*Jesus: "...if you pull up the weeds you might uproot the wheat along with
them. Let them grow together until harvest...." (Mt 13:29–30)*

---

[a] The word *'min'* literally means 'people' in general, but in this context it refers
to rulers in particular.—Translators.

[b] The word *'ch'u'* can have two entirely opposite connotations here: 1) clean,
well-tended, or lavishly arrayed, and 2) unclean, corrupt, or in disarray.
Although there is no way of determining which of these two meanings was
intended by Lao Tzu, the first has been chosen for reasons of textual consis-
tency.—Translators.

"INJUSTICE" RESOLVED.

The resolution to the anguish inherent in the lament "Why do the wicked prosper, while misfortune is the plight of the just?" lies outside the "field" of action: For Jesus, in future judgment; for Lao Tzu, in returning to the way of Tao.

But future judgment refers to present action. Orthodox theologian Thomas Hopko writes forcefully on the Christian imperative to redress injustice: "There is a great measure of injustice in the world: oppression, exploitation, inequality, tyranny. Some people have possessions and power and others are deprived and victimized. Some people are free to determine their destiny on earth, at least in certain external and social ways, while others are locked into their lot in life without the power of controlling, choosing or changing their ways of living and working. The Christian teaching is that injustice in all of its forms is rooted in wickedness and sin. It is not the result of some accident of history or biology. Where there is *injustice,* there is necessarily *guilt*....The fact that perfect justice will be established in the kingdom to come does not free human beings from establishing justice now, to the measure possible. On the contrary, it compels them to do so. 'But if any one has the world's goods and sees his brother in need, yet closes his heart against him, how does God's love abide in him? Little children, let us not love in word or in speech but in deed and in truth. (1 Jn 3:17–18)."[1]

E. M. Chen: "The *Tao Te Ching* definitely rejects the notion of election or predestination taught in some religions. The moral war, deadly serious though it is, is fought only on this side of existence. When Jesus said to let the wheat and weeds grow together until harvest time when the wheat will be gathered into the barn and the weeds burnt, he spoke of the kingdom of God as this world's ultimate achievement. Taoism shows that there is yet a deeper vision in which wheat and weeds are both gathered into the bosom of Tao, their sharp differences softened and blended into one."[2]

INTERIORITY.

Lao Tzu: "The five colors blind human eyes;
The five sounds deafen human ears;
The five flavors dull the human mouth...
Accordingly, the Sage cares for the stomach,
not for the eyes."[a] (TTC, 12)

"The Sage wears coarse clothing
And yet harbors jade within." (TTC, 70.)

Jesus: "The lamp of the body is your eye. When your eye is sound, then your whole body is filled with light, but when it is bad, then your body is in darkness. Take care, then, that the light in you not become darkness. If your whole body is full of light, and no part of it is in darkness, then it will be as full of light as a lamp illuminating you with its brightness." (Lk 11:34–36)

---

[a] 'Stomach' (*fu*) here symbolizes one's inner spirituality, while 'eyes' (*mu*) stands for externals.—Translators.

Thomas N. Hart: "The seeds of [God's] purpose are planted within us, and from within, in interaction with an environment that is also in God's hands, they would grow toward fullness of our possibilities."[1]

Huston Smith: "Though Tao is ultimately transcendent, it is also immanent. In this secondary sense it is the *way of the universe,* the norm, the rhythm, the driving power in all nature, the ordering principle behind all life. Behind, but also in the midst of all life, for when Tao enters this second mode it 'assumes flesh' and informs all things. It 'adapts its vivid essence, clarifies its manifold fullness, subdues its resplendent luster, and assumes the likeness of dust.' Basically spirit rather than matter, it cannot be exhausted; the more it is drawn upon, the more it flows, for it is 'that fountain ever on,' as Plotinus said of his counterpart of the Tao, his One."[2]

LEADERSHIP.

Lao Tzu: "The reason that the rivers and the seas,
Can become kings of one hundred valleys,
Is that they are adept [at taking] the lowly position,
Thus they become the kings of the one hundred valleys.
Accordingly, one who seeks to stand above the people,
Must in speech [and conduct] take the lower position;
One who seeks to lead the people,
Must first follow behind.
Accordingly, the Sage stands above,
and yet the people are not burdened;
Stands before them,
And yet they are not harmed.
Accordingly, the world rejoices in pushing the Sage forward,
Without tiring of it.
It is only because one does not compete,
That the world is not able to compete with one." (TTC, 66)

Chuang Tzu: "When Kuan Chung fell ill, Duke Huan went to inquire how he was. 'Father Chung,' he said, 'you are very ill. If—can I help but say it?—if your illness should become critical, then to whom should I entrust the affairs of the state?' Kuan Chung said, 'To whom would Your Grace like to entrust them?' 'Pao Shu-ya,' said the duke. 'That will never do! He is a fine man, a man of honesty and integrity. But he will have nothing to do with those who are not like himself. And if he once hears of someone's error, he won't forget it to the end of his days. If he were given charge of the state, he would be sure to tangle with you on the higher level and rile the people below him. It would be no time at all before he did something you considered unpardonable.' 'Well then, who will do?' asked the duke. 'If I must give an answer, then I would say that Hsi P'eng will do. He forgets those in high places and does not abandon those in low ones. He is ashamed that he himself is not like the Yellow Emperor, and pities those who are not like himself. He who shares his virtue with others is called a sage; he who shares his talents with others is called a worthy man. If he uses his worth in an attempt to oversee others, then he will never win their support; but if he uses it to humble himself before others, then he will never fail to win their support. With such a man, there are things within the state that he doesn't bother to hear about, things within the family that he doesn't bother to look after. If I must give an answer, I would say that Hsi P'eng will do.'" (Chapter 24, "Hsü Wu-Kuei")

Jesus: "Woe to you, scribes and Pharisees, you hypocrites. You lock the kingdom of heaven before human beings. You do not enter yourselves, nor do you allow entrance to those trying to enter." (Mt 23:13)

"For they preach but they do not practice. They tie up heavy burdens [hard to carry] and lay them on people's shoulders, but they will not lift a finger to move them. All their works are performed to be seen." (Mt 23: 3–5)

名與身孰親
身與貨孰多
得與亡孰病
是故甚愛
必大費
多藏必厚亡
知足不辱
知止不殆
可以長久

塈于彭宣

LEADERSHIP.

Michael R. Carey: "The gospel stories paint a consistent picture of how Jesus interacted with people, and this picture tells us a great deal about Christian leadership...the message is that the Messiah's method of making the kingdom of God present is to transform his followers into leaders who themselves serve as agents of moral growth and development for others. The symbol of leaven used in Jesus' parables typifies his leadership, which does not end in one leader–follower interaction but continues to spread, building a community of Christlike leaders—a kingdom of God."[1]

Arthur Waley instructs that an ideal Taoist leader creates in those under authority desired qualities and tendencies through the leader's exercise of *te*, or the virtue of Tao. Such "contagious" *te* is manifested in the qualities of simplicity, selflessness and detachment.[2]

Michael LaFargue: "With some leaders, every word they speak, every action they take, says, 'I am someone of great importance. You are my lowly subjects.' Such a person is an oppressive weight on the people, hurting them by casting them always in a bad light, as 'inferior.' People will not accept this. Weighed down, they weary of her. The people wearied, she loses their support. She becomes just one more individual, joining in society's quarrelsome competition for honor and status. (And she wonders why people become so contentious and quarrelsome with her.) Look at the ocean and the Yange–tze, greatest of rivers. Did they become great because of their talent for being impressive? No, their uniqueness among rivers lies in their surpassing lowness, occupying the place toward which all water naturally flows. This is an image of the weightless authority of the one who occupies the central place, but also the lowly place."[3]

"Ho-Shang Kung [d. 159 B.C.?] says, 'When the sage rules over the people, he doesn't oppress those below with his position. Thus the people uphold him and don't think of him as a burden. When he stands before them, he doesn't blind them with his glory. Thus the people love him as a parent and harbor no resentment. The sage is kind and loving and treats the people as if they were his children. Thus the whole world wants him for their leader. The people never grow tired of him because he doesn't struggle against them. Everyone struggles against something. But no one struggles against a person who doesn't struggle against anything.'"[4]

Ku-ying Ch'en: "If...the rulers choose to use laws and prohibitions to fetter the people—oppressing, taxing, and squeezing them—then it is no different from the whirlwinds and torrential rains in that it cannot endure long. Lao Tzu offers a very clear warning: tyrannical governments are evanescent.

"The consequences of administering a nation are similar to those described in the Chinese dictum, 'identical sounds respond to each other; identical attitudes seek each other out.' If those who rule are tranquil and 'nonactive' in their administration, then the people will respond with compliance and harmony. If those who rule are profligate and perverse, then the people will respond with resistance and distrust. If the integrity of the rulers is inadequate, then the people will respond with suspicion and duplicity."[5]

LIBERATING THE OPPRESSED.

Lao Tzu: "The Tao of Heaven in comparable to an outstretched bow:
When high, lower it;
When low, raise it;
When excessive, reduce it;
When deficient, supplement it.
The Tao of Heaven reduces what is excessive,
Supplements what is deficient...." (TTC, 77)

Jesus: "The Spirit of the Lord is upon me,
because he has anointed me
to bring glad tidings to the poor.
He has sent me to proclaim liberty to captives
and recovery of sight to the blind,
to let the oppressed go free,
and to proclaim a year acceptable to the Lord." (Lk 4:18–19)

LIBERATING THE OPPRESSED.

James W. Douglas: "The God whom Jesus addresses so intimately as 'Abba,' and the inauguration of whose reign on earth is the core of Jesus' message, is a God of Liberation....But this is a Liberator God-Man whose suffering resistance puts the flame of truth to injustice only after man has first sought Him in silence in the heat of the desert and fought with his Spirit in the freezing wind of the mountain's dark side. In the desert, on the sheer face of the mountain, man becomes God by renouncing power and becoming nothing. Now yin, now yang....The world changes."[1]

"Kao Heng [1900–] says, 'In attaching a string to a bow, we pull the bow down to attach the string to the top. We lift the bow up to attach the bottom. If the string is too long, we make it shorter. If the string is too short, we make it longer. This is exactly the way of Heaven.'"[2] Ku-ying Ch'en provides the application of the metaphor: "This chapter presents a comparison of the prevailing social conventions with the natural code which maintains the harmony of the cosmos. The natural code takes the surplus from that which has excess and subsidizes that which does not have enough, functioning on the principle that excess and deficiency are both equally harmful to natural phenomena. Ideally, the social code should imitate this principle, maintaining harmony and equality in the sphere of man.

"This however, is not the case. In human society, people who have power and position indulge themselves without consideration for the living conditions of the common people. Through heavy taxation the rich take from those who can least afford it, and the gap between rich and poor becomes increasingly wide. This imbalance, which seems to be a characteristic of most societies, does injury both ways—the rich and powerful become wasted and profligate while the impoverished people are under constant pressure to produce. Eventually, the situation reaches extreme proportions and explodes in revolution.

"As a solution to this seemingly endless cycle of ascendancy and sudden decline, Lao Tzu enjoins man to seek a pattern for his society in the natural order of the universe. When the Tao of man becomes one with the Tao of Heaven, all contention and destruction in human society will cease."[3]

LIFESPRING.

Lao Tzu: "Supreme goodness [Tao] is like water.
Water benefits the Ten Thousand Things,
And yet never competes with them." (TTC, 8)

*Jesus: "Let anyone who thirsts come to me and drink. Whoever believes
in me, as scripture says:
'Rivers of living water will flow from within him.'" (Jn 7:37–38)*

*"...whoever drinks the water I shall give will never thirst; the water I shall
give will become in him a spring of water welling up to eternal life." (Jn
4:14)*

Jesus was nurtured in a tradition in which water served as a profound and multivalent religious symbol: gift of God, source of paradisiacal fecundity, sign of divine favor, expression of supernatural goodness, graced life, purifying agent, abundance in the future fullness of time. Jesus took these themes upon himself.

Wing-Tsit Chan: "Water is perhaps the most outstanding among Lao Tzu's symbols for Tao. The emphasis of the symbolism is ethical rather than metaphysical or religious. It is interesting to note that, while early Indian philosophers associated water with creation and the Greek philosophers looked upon it as a natural phenomenon, ancient Chinese philosophers, whether Lao Tzu or Confucius, preferred to learn moral lessons from it. Broadly speaking, Western thought, derived chiefly from the Greeks, has been largely interested in metaphysical and scientific problems, Indian thought largely interested in religious problems, and Chinese thought largely interested in moral problems. It is not too much to say that these different approaches to water characterize the Western, the Indian, and the Chinese systems of thought."[1]

E. M. Chen: "The true fulfillment of the self is through fulfilling others. One who forgets the self is like water flowing downward to benefit all, collecting itself only at the lowest point shunned by others....To Confucius water was the symbol of intelligent activity: The wise rejoice in water, while the virtuous rejoice in the mountain (*Analects,* 6;21). The *Tao Te Ching* speaks of water as nearest to Tao for a different reason: by dwelling at the lowest places, water receives all the rejects of the world into itself. To dwell in lowly places shunned by the many is not a Confucian's choice....The role of the Taoist sage, on the other hand, is exactly to play the low ground, to receive all the filth under heaven (chapter 78;2). What is called superior goodness here, then, is the religious notion of goodness that transcends the ethical distinction between good and evil. It does not seek self-aggrandizement but self-donation."[2]

"Wu Ch'eng [1249–1333] says, 'Among those who follow the Tao, the best are like water: content to be on the bottom and, thus, free of blame. Most people hate being on the bottom and compete to be on the top; And when people compete, someone is maligned."[3]

LaFargue: "The fact that water flows downward and nourishes plants serves as an image illustrating the Taoist ideals of (a) not contending with others for high social status, (b) willingness to accept being in a low and unnoticed position ('which all others avoid'), and (c) devoting oneself to public service ('benefiting the thousands of things')...."[4]

上善若水　水善利萬物而不爭

處衆人之所惡　故幾於道

居善地　心善淵　與善仁

言善信　正善治

事善能　動善時

夫唯不爭

故無尤

一九九七
于書字

LIGHT IMAGERY.

Lao Tzu: "Make one's light [intellect] function;
Return to enlightenment [insight];
Invite no disaster in your life.
This is none other than
'Following the eternal (Tao).'" (TTC, 52)

Jesus: "Is a lamp brought in to be placed under a bushel basket or under a bed, and not to be placed on a lampstand? For there is nothing hidden except to be made visible; nothing is secret except to come to light." (Mk 4:21–22)

"...whoever lives the truth comes to the light, so that his works may be clearly seen as done in God." (Jn 3:21)

LIGHT IMAGERY.

St. Paul: "For you were once darkness, but now you are light in the Lord. Live as children of light, for light produces every kind of goodness and righteousness and truth." (Eph 5:8–9)

Christian liturgical and sacramental life witnesses to the symbolic power of light. Justin Martyr (second century) was the first of a long line of church theologians to refer to baptism as illumination or enlightenment. The white baptismal garment is referred to as the garment of light. The baptismal candle is lit from the Easter candle and given to the newly baptized with the admonition, "Receive the light of Christ."

Christ himself is described in the second article of the Nicene-Constantinopolitan Creed as the Son processing from the Father in the Trinity, "light from light, true God from true God." Light has also been associated with the dead. The prayer for them in the Roman canon asks for them a place of "light, happiness and peace." A common prayer for the dead asks that "perpetual light shine upon them."[1]

"Huai-Nan-Tzu [d. 122 B.C.] says, 'the light of the sun shines across the Four Seas but cannot penetrate a closed door or a covered window. While the light of the spirit reaches everywhere and nourishes everything.'"[2]

In *The Book of Balance and Harmony,* a famous anthology of writings by a thirteenth-century Taoist master of the School of Complete Reality, translated by Thomas Cleary: "The shining mind is always calm; in action, it responds to myriad changes. Even when active, it is essentially always calm...the shining mind is the mind of Tao...."[3]

Liu I-Ming (eighteenth century): "When lamplight shines inside a room, then the room is light while outside is dark. When the lamp is moved outside, then outside is light while inside the room is dark.

"What I realize as I observe this is the Tao of proper use of illumination.

"People's intellect and knowledge are like the light of a lamp. If that light is mistakenly used outside, in a contentious and aggressive manner, aiming for name and gain, scheming and conniving day and night, thinking a thousand thoughts, imagining ten thousand imaginings, chasing artificial objects and losing the original source, light on the outside but dark inside, this will go on until the body is injured and life is lost.

"If people give up artificiality and return to the real, dismiss intellectuality and cleverness, consider essential life the one matter of importance, practice inner awareness, refine the self and master the mind, observe all things with detachment so all that exists is empty of absoluteness, are not moved by external things and are not influenced by sensory experiences, being light inside and dark outside, they can thereby aspire to wisdom and become enlightened.

"Light that does not dazzle progresses to lofty illumination; therefore a classic says, 'The great sage appears ignorant, the great adept seems inept.'"[4]

Harold H. Oshima: "Light is another metaphor for the tao, and one that has special significance for the mirror metaphor of this *hsin* [mind]. The sage's relationship with the tao parallels the mirror's associations with sun and light. Just as the mirror can project light (in the case of the concave mirror, with remarkable results), the sage who has cleansed his bright mirror, 'whose inner being rests in the Great Serenity will send forth a Heavenly light' (Watson's translation of the *Chuang Tzu*, 254). The king who can successfully 'forget' will be the ruler who 'will shine mirror-like over the earth below'...(Watson, 154–155). As in the case of water metaphors, the *Chuang Tzu* makes numerous references to the special relationship between the sage, the *hsin,* and 'light.' Consequently, the sage 'who rides the clouds and mists' is also described as letting his 'spirit ascend and mount upon the light' (Watson, 33, 46, 137)."[5]

LIMITLESSNESS.

Lao Tzu: "The great Tao flows everywhere,
It may go left or right." (TTC, 34)

Jesus: "If you have faith the size of a mustard seed, you would say to [this] mulberry tree, 'Be uprooted and planted in the sea,' and it would obey you." (Lk 17:6)

LIMITLESSNESS.

The implications of the Christian commands to love God and neighbor are inexhaustible; but, so too, what can be accomplished through the application of faith is open-ended and far transcends what can be accomplished by mere human effort.

E. M. Chen: "...because Tao gave rise to all beings, it is truly the great. The greatness of Tao is in its effects...."
    Consciousness limits the creative act. Being unconscious, Tao's creativity is limitless."[1]

.

LOVE OF SELF, OTHERS.

Lao Tzu: "If one loves the world as one's body,[a]
One can be entrusted [to care for] the world." (TTC, 13)

Jesus: "You shall love your neighbor as yourself." (Mt 22:39)

---

[a] The Chinese character '*shen*,' literally 'body,' in this context signifies the selfish ego.—Translators.

LOVE OF SELF, OTHERS.

Each human being is constituted as both a subject and an object, a thinker and a thought about, an "I" and a "self." The "I" that is me can come to know my self, love my self, hate my self, doubt my self, betray my self, pity my self, punish my self, justify my self, feel my self to be elated, guilty, bored, tired, confused, moved by emotion, etc. I can contemplate the self-image I project to others, and I can order my life with the intention of self-improvement. In short, humans are the most self-conscious of beings. The relation between loving one's self and loving others is such that the capability to do the latter is predicated on the reality of the former. One may have undeniably strong feelings for another, but without love of self, true love it is not. (Modern psychological literature speaks of emotional attachment to another or others issuing apart from a fundamental love of self as "dysfunctional codependency.") The Catholic philosopher Jean Guitton suggested that the entire Bible can be summed up with the single sentence: "Je crois à l'Amour"—I believe in love.[1] That Jesus can and did *command* his followers to love is a recognition of the conative rather than emotional character of Christian love, for it is only the will, not feelings, that can be so summoned. Revelation teaches that each "I" that can exercise the will to love is created in the "image and likeness" of God, i.e., it is a mystery—even to one's self. St. Paul, in his letter to the Galatians, named for each Christian the mystery of postbaptismal I-dentity: " Yet I live, no longer I, but Christ lives in me." (Gal 2:20)

The Christian imperative to love is exclusive of any expectations or demands to be loved in return. Indeed, on this side of the kingdom where the still-prayed-for universal reign of God is yet to be fully revealed in the hearts of all people, to love is to place oneself at risk of everything from misunderstanding to rejection to death. This fact of life is not to dissuade the believer from imaging Jesus' sacrificial love. Joseph Needham reflects on this point: "I have spoken already about cosmic love and love among us at the human level, but love is vulnerable, inevitably doomed to suffering, if it were only on account of the terrible fact of transience itself. There is rejection, there is unkindness, there is cruelty, there is evanescence, there is coldness. Anything may happen. In our religion we believe that Christ dared to let go and emptied himself of divine glory when he, the Tao, became incarnate in human body. Love was denied, love was betrayed, love was crucified—and love was undefeated. That was the 'Way' [Tao] of the cross. That was the Truth about human relationships, and that was the Life which all men and women must lead if patterns of the Tao are to be fulfilled on earth. And so we come back to our starting point and look again at the Way or Tao of love expressed in that wonderful collect: 'O God, who has taught us that all our doings without love are nothing worth, send down thy Holy Spirit and pour into our hearts that most excellent gift of love, the very bond of peace and of all virtues, without which whosoever liveth is counted dead before Thee.'"[2]

Chung-yuan Chang teaches that in Taoism, compassionate, universal and nondiscriminatory love is inseparable from renunciation (ch'ien): "When love is measured or gradated according to objective conditions, rational discrimination and determination destroy direct, immediate fellow feeling. Therefore, Taoists declare that when *jen,* or gradation of love, is discarded, people will love each other once again. Taoist love is based upon *t'zu,* or compassion. It is spontaneity and sincerity derived from the concealment of love and is free from any artificial effort. When one has *t'zu,* one naturally renounces unnecessary, manmade glories and extravagances. Thus, the principle of *ch'ien* takes place."[3]

寵辱若驚貴大患
若身何謂寵辱若驚
寵為下得之若驚
失之若驚是謂寵
辱若驚何謂貴大患
若身吾所以有大患
者為吾有身及吾
無身吾有何患故
貴身身為天下若可
寄天下愛以身為
天下若可託天下

MEEKNESS/HUMILITY.

Lao Tzu: "The reason that the rivers and the seas,
Can become kings of one hundred valleys.
Is that they are adept [at taking] the lowly position,
Thus they become the kings of one hundred valleys.
Accordingly, one who seeks the stand above the people,
Must in speech [and conduct] take the lower position;
One who seeks to lead the people,
Must first follow behind." (TTC, 66)

"Accordingly, the Sage embraces the One
and becomes the model of the world;
Does not flaunt itself,
And therefore is affirmed;
Does not boast,
And therefore merit is self-evident;
Does not assert self-importance,
And therefore endures." (TTC, 22)

"Accordingly, the Sage accomplishes the task
And yet claims not credit,
Succors them and yet does not appropriate them;
He does not wish to display his worth."[a] (TTC, 77)

*Jesus: "Blessed are the meek,
for they will inherit the land." (Mt 5:5)*

*"Whoever exalts himself will be humbled; but whoever humbles himself
will be exalted." (Mt 23:12)*

---

[a] According to some textual critics, the last sentence of this chapter is a later
interpolation and should not appear in this chapter.—Translators.

Michael Coogan instructs that this beatitude that describes the meek as inheritors of the land is clearly derived from Psalms 37:11, and Jesus probably intended its original, concrete sense. But in view of Matthew's spiritualization of this and the other beatitudes, the meek seem to be those who are not only socioeconomically deprived but patiently accepting of their status as well.[1]

St. Paul: "Rather, God chose the foolish of the world to shame the wise, and God chose the weak of the world to shame the strong, and God chose the lowly and despised of the world, those who count for nothing, to reduce to nothing those who are something, so that no human being might boast before God. It is due to him that you are in Christ Jesus, who became for us wisdom from God, as well as righteousness, sanctification, and redemption, so that, as it is written, 'Whoever boasts, should boast in the Lord.'" (1 Cor 1:26–31)

St. Isaac of Syria, from the *Philokalia,* Sentences 112 to 115: "A truly humble man not only does not wish to be seen or known by others, but more, his will is to plunge away from himself into himself, to become nothing, as if not existing, not yet come into being....A humble man protects himself from all the multiple, and thus remains in stillness, quiet, peace, modesty and reverence....Nothing can ever surprise, disturb, or dismay him....A humble man does not dare even to pray or petition God about something, and does not know what to ask for; he simply keeps his senses silent and waits only for mercy and for whatever the Most Worshipful Majesty may be pleased to send him. When he bows down with his face to the earth, and the inner eyes of his heart are raised to the gates of the Holy of Holies, where He dwells Whose abode is—darkness, before Whom the Seraphims close their eyes, he dares only to speak and pray thus: 'May Thy will be done upon me, O Lord!'"[2]

St. Francis de Sales taught that spiritual progress is impossible without the cultivation of this virtue: "One of the good uses that we should learn to make of gentleness is in things which concern ourselves, never upsetting ourselves about our imperfections; for though reason requires that, when we are at fault, we should be displeased and sorry, yet we must prevent ourselves from having a displeasure which is bitter, sulky, spiteful and angry. Many people commit a great fault because, when they have given way to anger, they are annoyed for being annoyed and angry at having been angry and upset; for this is the way they keep their hearts preserved and steeped in anger...."[3]

"Wang Chen [fl. 809] says, 'Through humility the sage gains the approval of the people. Once he gains their approval, he gains their tireless support. And once he gains their tireless support, struggling over rank naturally comes to an end.'"[4]

"Jen Fa-Jung [1930–] says, 'Whenever the sage goes in the world, he acts humble and withdrawn and blends in with others. He treats everyone, noble or common, rich or poor, with the same kindness and equality. His mind merges with theirs. Ordinary people concentrate on what they hear and see and concern themselves with their own welfare. The sage's mind is like that of a newborn baby, pure and impartial.'"[5]

Huston Smith: "[Taoists'] almost reverential attitude toward humility led the Taoists to honor hunchbacks and cripples because of the way they typified meekness and self-effacement. They were fond of pointing out that the value of cups, windows, and doorways lies in the parts of them that are not there. 'Selfless as melting ice' is one of their descriptive figures."[6]

絕聖棄智民利百倍絕仁棄義民復孝慈絕巧棄利盜賊無有此三言以為文不足故令有所屬見素抱樸少私寡欲絕學無憂

NONATTACHMENT.

Lao Tzu: "Name or self—which is more to be prized?
Self or goods—which is more to be valued?
Gain or loss—which is to be considered more harmful?
Therefore, excessive frugality must lead to great waste;
Excessive accumulation must lead to heavy losses.
Knowing what is sufficient delivers one from dishonor;
Knowing when to stop delivers one from disaster,
Allowing one to endure for long." (TTC, 44)

Jesus: "What profit would there be for one to gain the whole world and forfeit his life?" (Mt 16:26)

NONATTACHMENT.

Because God's kingdom is a divine grace—a gift—common criteria for human achievement are inappropriate and misleading when applied to it.[1] The sense of detachment, or nonattachment that the kingdom requires for its reception is a major concept in the history of Christian spirituality. Margaret Miles writes: "Meister Eckhart, a fourteenth-century German mystic, describes detachment as a process of stripping oneself of everything that defends or conceals the centre or 'core of the soul,' the place of experience and knowledge of God. His agenda of identifying and relinquishing habits, rituals and practices, social conditioning, feelings and ideas is preliminary to a spontaneous regathering of these in constellation around a new centre of the self which has been constituted by the experience of God. After this process of stripping and gathering, Eckhart taught, the person will be less likely to *identify* herself or himself with either objects or relationships. Eckhart's description of the meaning and importance of detachment is characteristic of many spiritual leaders. His insistence that, when one is not attached to characteristic patterns of thought and behavior, created goods no longer prevent but actually 'point you to God,' is an important correction of the view that the need to reject implies a pejorative estimation of the goodness and beauty of creation and other human beings."[2]

St. Abba Dorotheus, from the *Philokalia:* "We should not be disturbed even when passion [read 'attachment'] troubles us. Why be surprised, passionate man, and why be disturbed when passion stirs you? You yourself have fashioned it and consent to keep it in yourself—and yet you are disturbed? You have accepted its tokens and you say: why does it trouble me? It is better for you to endure, strive and pray God to help you; for it is impossible for a man who obeyed passions, not to have painful attacks of them. Their vessels, as Abba Sisoy said, are within you; give them back their token and they will leave you. Since we have loved them and brought them into action, it is impossible for us not to be enticed by passionate thoughts, which urge us, even against our will, to obey passions, because we have voluntarily surrendered ourselves into their hands."[3]

Lee Yearley contrasts Taoist nonattachment with the equanimity derived from philosophical Stoicism: "Detachment in the radical Chuang Tzu is considerably more subtle. Unlike the conventional view, you do not say, 'That's the way it is, like it or not.' Rather you say, 'That's the way it should be' or 'That's the only imaginable way it can be.' Most important, the crucial notion is not that mind dispels emotion by its possession of a general perspective. Rather the crucial notion is that the mind holds to and lets go of events as they arise, pass before you, and disappear. You hold to each moment, you are attached to it, but the attachment to any particular offense does not persevere. The attitude Chuang-tzu commends is a complex mixture of attachment and detachment. A total involvement with each moment and enjoyment of it combine with a detachment from the moment once it passes and a lack of desire that it return."[4]

LaFargue, in assuming the persona of a Taoist commentator, offers the following paraphrase of chapter 44 of the *Tao Te Ching:* "It might seem that, when you acquire more possessions or make a name for yourself, you are 'adding' to what you are—all you need to worry about is losing these things. But the real problem lies in gaining, not in losing. In attaching so much importance to gaining these things, you are really just expending energy and wearing yourself out, making your existence anxious and precarious by staking so much on what can easily be lost. You should learn to stop this flow of your energy outward, and to rest content in you own being. This is ultimate security."[5]

視之不見名曰夷 聽之不聞名曰希 搏之不得名曰微

NONCONFORMITY.

Lao Tzu: "To know [Tao], yet [appear] not to know, is best." (TTC, 71)

"[My] words have a ground [in Tao];
[My] deeds have a guide [in Tao].
Only, due to the lack of knowledge [of Tao]
None understand me." (TTC, 70)

"Oh, mine is a fool's mind,
so muddled and i-gnorant!" [a] (TTC, 20)

"What benefit in conforming your behavior to someone's conventions?
It violates your nature and dissipates your energy.
Why separate your spiritual life and your practical life? To an integral being, there is no distinction." (HHC, 50)

Jesus: "The sabbath was made for man, not man for the sabbath." (Mk 2:27)

"Have you not read what David did when he and his companions were hungry, how he went into the house of God and ate the bread of offering, which neither he nor his companions but only the priests could lawfully eat?...I say to you, something greater than the temple is here....For the Son of Man is Lord of the sabbath." (Mt 12:3–8)

---

[a] The word 'i-gnorant' is used here in the sense of 'ignosis,' that is, nonknowledge. The hyphen conveys the inherent paradox of Taoist thought. In Lao Tzu's view, the Taoist mind appears to be that of a fool to the unenlightened. In truth, however, it represents a profound identity with Tao.—Translators.

NONCONFORMITY.

The sabbath activities of Jesus (Cf. Mt 12:1–8 and 9–14, Mk 1:21–28, Lk 13:10–17 and 14:1–6, and Jn 3:1–18 and 9:1–41) which are reflective of his relation to religious law in general, were neither hurtful provocations nor mere protests against legal restrictions, but were integral to Jesus' essential proclamation of the inbreaking of the kingdom of God as manifestation of God's freedom, healing and rulership.[1]

If the term "understanding" in the following commentary on chapter 71 of the *Tao Te Ching* is limited to the erroneous common understandings of those who were scandalized by Jesus' actions and attitudes, then the commentary obtains even in the Christian context:

"Li Hsi-chai [fl. 1167] says, 'Understanding depends on things, hence it involves fabrication. Not understanding returns to the origin, hence it approaches the truth. If someone can understand that not understanding approaches the truth and that understanding involves fabrication, they are transcendent. If they don't understand that understanding involves fabrication and vainly increase their understanding, they use the affliction as the medicine. Only by understanding that understanding is affliction can one be free of affliction. This is why the sage is not afflicted.'"[2]

And, it may be added, this is why the sage is free.

81

NONCONTENTION/PACIFISM.

Lao Tzu: "Supreme goodness [Tao] is like water.
Water benefits the Ten Thousand Things,
And yet never competes with them." (TTC, 8)

"Being audaciously brave invites death;
Being non-audaciously brave promotes life.
Of these two, one is beneficial, the other harmful.
What [the Tao of] Heaven detests, who knows the reason?
Accordingly, even the Sage feels this is difficult.
The Tao of Heaven does not compete, and yet is adept at overcoming;
Does not speak, and yet is adept at responding;
Spontaneously comes forth without being beckoned;
Seemingly idle, and yet is adept at planning." (TTC, 73)

*"[Jesus] withdrew from that place. Many [people] followed him, and he
cured them all, but he warned them not to make him known. This was
to fulfill what had been spoken through Isaiah the prophet:
'...He will not contend or cry out,
nor will anyone hear his voice in the streets.
A bruised reed he will not break,
a smoldering wick he will not quench,
until he brings justice to victory.
And in his name the Gentiles will hope.'" (Mt 12:15–21)*

NONCONTENTION/PACIFISM.

Daniel A. Dombrowski, in his work in defense of Christian pacifism, notes that "pacifism is not strictly speaking 'passive' in the pejorative sense of the term, but a disciplined attempt to attain what we have seen Whitehead call 'that Harmony of Harmonies which calms destructive turbulence....'"[1]

Ku-ying Ch'en: "Lao Tzu considers that the laws of nature are flexible in the sense that they are conducive to the natural development of all things. Further, these laws preserve a balance in the cosmos in which all things are complementary each to the other. As such, they do not allow contention or conflict. Man, in his conduct, should seek to emulate these laws, avoiding any actions which might lead to contention. If one's 'courage lies in tenacity,' he will make a display of solidity and firmness and assert himself in dealing with others. If, on the other hand, one's 'courage lies in diffidence,' he will be submissive and unassuming. It is only through being submissive and unassuming that all people in the society can develop in compliance with their natures, and that conflict and disorder can be averted."[2]

"Li Hung-Fu [fl. 1574] says, 'How do we know the best do not compete? Everyone else chooses nobility. They alone choose humility. Everyone else chooses the pure. They alone choose the base. What they choose is what everyone else hates. Who is going to compete with them?'"[3]

NONEXCLUSIVENESS.

Lao Tzu: "Tao is the sanctuary of the Ten Thousand Things.
It is treasured by good people,
While the nongood must rely on it as well....
Even if a person is not good, why should [Tao] abandon them?"
(TTC, 62)

"The first practice is the practice of undiscriminating virtue:
take care of those who are deserving;
also, and equally, take care of those who are not.
When you extend your virtue in all directions without discriminating,
your feet are firmly planted on the
path that returns to the Tao." (HHC, 2)

"If you attach yourself to gross energies—loving this
person, hating that clan, rejecting one experience or
habitually indulging in another—then you will lead a series of heavy,
attached lives." (HHC, 34)

*Jesus: "...[the Father] makes his sun rise on the bad and the good, and
causes rain to fall on the just and the unjust." (Mt 5:45)*

*"Amen, I say to you, tax collectors and prostitutes are entering the king-
dom of God before you." (Mt 21:31)*

NONEXCLUSIVENESS.

Arnold Yeung: "The universality and impartiality of Tao should remind Christians of the reality and objectivity of the indwelling Christ that constitutes new life, the ground and actuality of the union with God. The Christian needs constantly to be reminded that no sin can annihilate the solidarity between God and his people, brought about by the life and death of Jesus Christ. The wickedness of humanity, though costly to the Redeemer, is not mighty enough to crush the redeemed...."[1]

NONJUDGMENT.

Chuang Tzu: "Duke Ai of Lu said to Confucius, 'In Wei there was an ugly man named Ai T'ai-T'o. But when men were around him, they thought only of him and couldn't break away, and when women saw him, they ran begging to their fathers and mothers, saying, "I'd rather be this gentleman's concubine that another man's wife!"—there were more than ten such cases and it hasn't stopped yet...He wasn't in the position of a ruler where he could save other men's lives, and he had no store of provisions to fill men's bellies. On top of that, he was ugly enough to astound the whole world, chimed in but never led, and knew no more than what went on right around him. And yet men and women flocked to him. He certainly must be different from other men, I thought, and I summoned him so I could have a look. Just as they said—he was ugly enough to astound the world. But he hadn't been with me more than a month or so when I began to realize what kind of man he was, and before the year was out, I really trusted him. There was no one in the state to act as chief minister, and I wanted to hand the government over to him. He was vague about giving an answer, evasive, as though he hoped to be let off, and I was embarrassed, but in the end I turned the state over to him. Then, before you knew it, he left me and went away. "I felt completely crushed, as though I'd suffered a loss and didn't have anyone left to enjoy my state with. What kind of man is he anyway?'" (Chapter 5, "The Sign of Virtue Complete.")

Jesus: "Stop judging by appearances, but judge justly." (Jn 7:24)

"You judge by appearances, but I do not judge anyone." (Jn 8:15)

St. Abba Dorotheus, from the *Philokalia:* "It is one thing to speak evil, and another to condemn or disparage. To speak evil means to say of a man: he lied, or committed adultery, or was angry or did some wrong. So saying, a man speaks evil of his brother, that is, speaks passionately of his transgression. But to condemn means saying: so and so is a liar, an adulterer, a bad-tempered man. Such a man condemns the very disposition of another's soul, passes judgment on his whole life, in saying that he is such and such, and condemning him as such. And this is a grievous sin.

"The Pharisee, when praying and thanking God for his virtues, did not lie but spoke the truth and was not condemned for this; for we must thank God when it is given us to do something good, since He has helped and assisted us in this. It was not for this he was condemned, nor for saying 'I thank thee, that I am not as other men.' But when he turned to the publican as said, 'or even this publican' he incurred condemnation. For he condemned the person as such, the very disposition of his soul, his entire life. This is why the publican was 'justified rather than the other' (Lk 18:11, 14)."[1]

Ai-thai Tho does not possess physical beauty at all but both men and women love him. He does not have social status or money, but the king respected him and nominated him as prime minister. After he left the king, the king felt there was no joy, and no other one deserving of his trust. Inner beauty, rather than external appearance, is the more essential and valuable.

Alan K. L. Chan: "The knowledge of the sage, in other words, has nothing to do with outward appearances or trivial details; rather it has to do with inner structure, with the 'nature' of things. And what makes this kind of knowledge possible is precisely the idea of a 'principle' that characterizes the workings of the Way...."[2]

NONREVENGE.

Lao Tzu: "Repay resentment with virtue." (TTC, 63)

Jesus: "You have heard that it was said,
'An eye for an eye and a tooth for a tooth.'
But I say to you,
offer no resistance to one who is evil.
When someone strikes you on [your] right cheek,
turn the other one to him as well." (Mt 5:38–39)

NONREVENGE.

Is Jesus recommending the most strategically effective means to gain the high moral ground so as to shame the offender into admitting defeat? The preference here is to believe that the reference and recommendation is a response that contextualizes the harsh action with all other actions and relationships: the one struck, in so acting, turns the attention of both himself/herself and the one who strikes to the infinitely wide horizon of the kingdom's peace within which the gravity of the issue that caused the aggression is relativized.

Jurgen Moltmann: "Whoever accepts the law of retaliation in regard to the enemy falls into the vicious circle from which there is not escape; one is inevitably the enemy of one's enemy, and the hostility determines the nature of the relationship. If evil is repaid with evil, then the one evil always focuses on the other evil, because only in this way can it justify its hostility and right to retaliate...The attitude toward the enemy that Jesus puts in place of deterrence is 'love of enemy' (Mt 5:43ff). What is meant by that under the conditions of the nuclear age? Love of enemy is not retaliation, but creative love. Whoever repays evil with good no longer retaliates but creates something new."[1]

E. M. Chen comments that Lao Tzu teaches that the proper response to violent action is exposure to the pristine condition of nature unburdened with distinctions between good and evil. Within the moral sphere, distinguishing good from evil can be no resolution of the problem of evil. Only when humans transcend virtue to the level of nature prior to the good/evil distinction can one be free from evil. *Yuan,* injury or wrong, also means rancor. Primal nature bears no rancor, accepts and suffers injury, heals injury such that there is no trace of injury left. Further, nature prior to virtue is the state of abiding suppleness, and natural healing. Lao Tzu is calling for a return to the state when problems have not arisen because the conditions producing problems were not yet activated by willful assertion; a time when the great is yet small, the much is yet little; when injuries have not yet appeared since all beings, in their primal state, are in union with all.[2]

Holmes Welch, in splitting the difference between Christianity and Taoism in reference to this theme, imputes a "purposive" intent to Lao Tzu: "Is this the same doctrine as our Christian Quietism, in which we turn the other cheek? It is not. A Christian returns good for evil in the spirit of self-abnegation, as a holy duty, and as an expression of his love for God and fellow man. Ostensibly, Lao Tzu would have us return good for evil...because that is the most effective technique of getting people to do what we want."[3]

NONVIOLENCE.

Lao Tzu: "Whoever assists the ruler with Tao,
Does not dominate the world by force of arms.
The use of force tends to invite requital.
Wherever armies are stationed,
Briars and thorns grow." (TTC, 30)

"Weapons and armaments are tools of ill omen,
Things detested by all.
Therefore, whoever has Tao turns away from them
The noble when at home honor the left;[a]
When at war, they honor the right.[b]
Weapons and armaments are tools of illomen,
Not tools for the noble.
If using them is unavoidable,
The best policy is calm restraint.
Victory is not worthy of praise,
So whoever praises[c] it takes pleasure in slaughter...
War is to be treated as a funeral rite.
After multitudes have been slaughtered,
Weep with sorrowful grief;
After the victory,
Observe the occasion with funeral rites."[d] (TTC, 31)

"A good soldier[e] is never vicious;
A good fighter is never enraged;
a good victor wins the enemy over by avoiding strife;
A good manager lowers his position.
This is called 'the virtue of noncontention';
This is called 'managerial strength':
The is called "matching age-old Heaven's ultimacy.""[f] (TTC, 68)

Jesus: "Put your sword back into its sheath, for all who take the sword will perish by the sword." (Mt 26:52)

---

^a 'The left' symbolizes the place of good omens.—Translators.

^b 'The right' symbolizes the place of bad omens.—Translators.

^c 'Praise' is a derived meaning for the original Chinese, *'mei,'* literally 'beauty' or 'to beautify.' Hence, an alternative translation here is: 'To win [the battle] is not beautiful,/ So whoever beautifies it takes pleasure in slaughter.'—Translators.

^d These lines seem to be an interpolation; cf. Wing-tsit Chan, *The Way of Lao Tzu,* 156.—Translators.

^e An alternative translation of the word 'shih,' based on Wang Pi's commentary, is 'officer' (one who leads soldiers).—Translators.

^f The textual critic Yü Yüe contends that the word *ku,* meaning 'age-old' or 'ancient,' is a later interpolation. In any case, the 'ultimacy' (*chi*) of 'Heaven' (*t'ien*) or 'Heaven of old' (*t'ien-ku*) apparently refers to Tao itself.—Translators.

大成若缺其用不弊
大盈若沖其用不窮

NONVIOLENCE.

Thomas Merton: "One of the missions of Christian nonviolence is to restore a different standard of practical judgment in social conflicts. This means that Christian humility of nonviolent action must establish itself in the minds and memories of modern man not only as *conceivable* and possible, but as a *desirable alternative* to what he now considers the only realistic possibility: namely political technique backed by force. Here the human dignity of nonviolence must manifest itself clearly in terms of a freedom and a nobility which are able to resist political manipulation and brute force and show them up as arbitrary, barbarous and irrational. This will not be easy....The realism of nonviolence must be made evident by humility and self-restraint which clearly show frankness and open-mindedness and invite the adversary to serious and reasonable discussion."[1]

Lisa Sowle Cahill: "The kingdom is both present or immanent in our experience, and transcendent in that it is graciously enabled by the saving inauguration of a new divine-human interaction, a mutually responsive relationship profoundly beyond human creation or control. The question of violence, then, turns not on whether a new life is only partly possible now, because the kingdom is moving in a linear progression toward a future greater fulfillment. Pacifism as a mode of Christian discipleship depends on whether, in presently living out of the kingdom-as-reality, we see, trust, and lay hold of a judging but sustaining power that enables us to respond to the 'other'—stranger, friend, or enemy—with the compassionate, enfolding love that is God's."[2]

Ku-ying Ch'en: "'Warlike emotions' and 'anger' are both aggressive sentiments, being expressions of violence. Lao Tzu opposes such displays, fearing these sentiments might lead people to find perverse pleasure in battle and killing...The commencement of hostilities means aggression has reared its head. The most effective method of dealing with aggression is to give it room in which to dissolve itself. Since aggression is a mutation of natural potential, it will die of its own accord unless we inadvertently provide it with an environment in which to grow....Given the situation in which it is absolutely necessary to respond to aggressors with military action, the leaders of the nation should 'treat this affair as a funeral ceremony.' When people are being slaughtered because of the wanton ambitions of a few, this is reason indeed to mourn. Even when the military engagements are victorious, there is not reason for elation—there is no glory and victory in war. This is the voice of humanism which colors Lao Tzu's philosophy."[3]

NONWORRY.

Lao Tzu: "There is an origin in the world,[a]
Which is the Mother of the world.
Once we know the Mother,
We can know the children,[b]
We return to embrace the Mother.
Throughout one's lifetime,
One will be delivered from danger." (TTC, 52)

Jesus: "Therefore I tell you, do not worry about your life, what you will eat [or drink], or about your body, what you will wear. Is not life more than food and the body more than clothing? Look at the birds in the sky; they do not sow or reap, they gather nothing into barns, yet your heavenly Father feeds them. Are not you more important than they? Can any of you by worrying add a single moment to your life-span? Why are you anxious about clothes? Learn from the way the wild flowers grow. They do not work or spin. But I tell you that not even Solomon in all his splendor was clothed like one of them. If God so clothes the grass of the field, which grows today and is thrown into the oven tomorrow, will he not much more provide for you, O you of little faith? So do not worry and say 'What are we to eat?' or 'What are we to drink?' or 'What are we to wear?' All these things the pagans seek. Your heavenly Father knows that you need them all. But seek first the kingdom [of God] and his righteousness, and all these things will be given you besides. Do not worry about tomorrow; tomorrow will take care of itself." (Mt 6:25–34)

---

[a] In distinction from other translations, the metaphorical use of the word 'origin' (*shih*) here signifies the ontological, rather than temporal, priority of Tao as Origin (No-thingness) over the Ten Thousand Things (Being).—Translators.
[b] The term 'children' is used here in a metaphorical sense and stands for the Ten Thousand Things.—Translators.

NONWORRY.

The subject at hand is not whether or not one has a sense of responsibility with regard to the provision of daily needs; rather, it is whether one has the appropriate sense of priority with regard to the requirements of God's kingdom. Faith, or trust in God the provider, supersedes preoccupation with how one looks in the opinion of others or the quality and quantity of food one may have become accustomed to consume. (That Jesus is addressing those enjoying Galilean prosperity is to be assumed).

E. M. Chen: "The overall message is the importance for consciousness to revert to the unconscious as its source. Only that form of life which is rooted in the source or mother is truly illumined (*ming*) and long-lasting (*ch'ang*)."[1]

OF LIFE, DEATH, AND THE LOGIC OF REVERSION.

Lao Tzu: "Flexibility preserves wholeness;
Bending leads to straightness;
Hollowness leads to fullness;
Wearing out leads to renewal;
Deficit leads to gain;
Plentitude leads to perplexity." (TTC, 22)

Chuang Tzu: "Life is the companion of death, death is the beginning of life. Who understands their workings? A person's life is a coming-together of breath. If it comes together, there is life; if it scatters, there is death. And if life and death are companions to each other, then what is there for us to be anxious about?

The Ten Thousand Things are really one. We look on some as beautiful because they are unearthly; we look on others as ugly because they are foul and rotten. But from the foul and rotten the rare and unearthly are born, and the rare and unearthly upon death turn into the foul and rotten. So it is said, you have only to comprehend the one breath that is the world. The sage never ceases to value oneness." (Chapter 22, "Knowledge Wandered North")

Jesus: "...many who are first will be last, and the last will be first." (Mt 19:30)

*"Blessed are you who are poor,
for the kingdom of God is yours.
Blessed are you who are now hungry,
for you will be satisfied.
Blessed are you who are now weeping,
for you will laugh.
Blessed are you when people hate you,
and when they exclude and insult you,*

and denounce your name as evil
on account of the Son of Man.
Rejoice and leap for joy on that day! Behold, your reward will be great in
heaven. For their ancestors treated the prophets in the same way.
But woe to you who are rich,
for you have received your consolation.
But woe to you who are filled now,
for you will be hungry.
Woe to you who laugh now,
for you will grieve and weep.
Woe to you when all speak well of you,
for their ancestors treated the false prophets in this way." (Lk 6:20–26)

"For whoever wishes to save his life will lose it, but whoever loses his life
for my sake will save it." (Lk 9:24)

"Amen, amen, I say to you, unless a grain of wheat falls to the ground
and dies, it remains just a grain of wheat; but if it dies, it produces much
fruit." (Jn 12:24)

三十輻共一轂
當其無，有
車之用
埏埴以為
器當其
無有器
之用鑿
戶牖以為室
當其無，有室之用
故有之以為利
無之以為用

于彭
一九九七年

OF LIFE, DEATH, AND THE LOGIC OF REVERSION.

With regard to the beatitudes, the difference between Christian and Taoist applications of the "logic of reversion" is one of intent. Jesus's intent was, in part, consolation; that of the Lao Tzu was to inculcate the philosophical perspective that is conducive to living in Tao-harmony.

One of the fundamental differences between Taoist and Christian worldviews is that for Taoism, existence is played out in unending *cycles* of reversions that include the most fundamental pair: Being and Non-Being.

Living in Tao-harmony and living out the Christian ethos exhibit close similarity when fullness-of-life and death-to-self are the terms of reversion. Self-emptying, dying to self (not out of self-hatred, but as the offering of what is most precious for an even greater sake) in order to live, is a master theme in the Christian faith. St. Paul wrote thus: "Have among yourselves the same attitude that is also yours in Christ Jesus, / Who, though he was in the form of God, did not regard equality with God something to be grasped. / Rather, he emptied himself, taking the form of a slave, coming in human likeness; and found human in appearance, / he humbled himself, becoming obedient to death, even death on a cross. Because of this, God greatly exalted him and bestowed on him the name that is above every name..." (Phil 2:5–9). Upon being baptized into the infinitely larger death/life of Christ ("We were indeed buried with him through baptism into death, so that, just as Christ was raised from the dead by the glory of the Father, we too might live in newness of life"—Rom 6:4) into the larger "I" ("Yet I live, no longer I, but Christ lives in me"—Gal 2:20), it is the daily project of each Christian to live out the mystery of death/new life.

St. Maximus the Confessor: "The end of the present life is wrongly, I think, called death, but rather is it the liberation from death, escape from the realm of corruption, freedom from slavery, cessation of tribulations, end of battles, way out of darkness, rest from labors, the calming of agitation, protection from shame, escape from passions and, generally speaking, the end of all evils; the saints gained all these things, making themselves strangers and pilgrims on earth by refashioning themselves through freely self-inflicted death."[1]

OUTREACH.

Lao Tzu: "[Supreme Goodness] dwells in what vulgar people spurn,
That is why it approximates the Tao." (TTC, 8)

"Who can enjoy enlightenment and remain indifferent to suffering in the world?
This is not in keeping with the Way.
Only those who increase their service along with their understanding can be called men and women of Tao." (HHC, 53)

Jesus: "Those who are well do not need a physician, but the sick do." (Mt 9:12)

"The tax collectors and sinners were all drawing near to listen to him, but the Pharisees and scribes began to complain, saying, 'This man welcomes sinners and eats with them.'" (Lk 15:1–2)

"I did not come to call the righteous but sinners." (Mk. 2:17)

OUTREACH.

The literally low, or last, public spaces in Jesus' society were reserved for the religiously "lost" or marginalized, a social stratum that included the public sinner, the sick and the poor. Although incurring ritual impurity in the eyes of the strictly law-observant for doing so, Jesus displayed a marked preference for keeping company in such places and issuing admission to the kingdom to those who dwelt there. Sacramental theologian Regis Duffy, O.F.M., comments: "If Jesus ate with sinners as a witness to God's offer of reconciliation, how can his church do any less? Today we use the term *outreach* to describe service that extends past our usual boundaries. There is the lesson the eucharist constantly teaches the community: to reach out creatively to the 'unacceptable' and the 'undesirable' with a compassion and service that bespeaks the Master criticized for his table companions."[1]

"Ho-shang Kung [d. 159 B.C.?] says, 'The best people have a nature like that of water. They're like mist or dew in the sky, like a stream or a spring on land. Most people hate moist or muddy places, places where water alone dwells. The nature of water is like the Tao: empty, clear and deep. As water empties, it gives life to others. It reflects without becoming impure, and there is nothing it cannot wash clean. Water can take any shape, and it is never out of touch with the seasons. How could anyone malign something with such qualities as this.'"[2]

PEACEMAKERS.

Lao Tzu: "Hold onto the great image,
And all the world will come.
All come and meet with no harm,
And thus, [enjoy] peace and security." (TTC, 35)

*Jesus: "Blessed are the peacemakers,
for they will be called children of God." (Mt 5:9)*

PEACEMAKERS.

The sense of detachment and poverty of spirit links co-naturally with being a person of peace. Henri Nouwen made the relationship explicit: "How can I be a man of peace?... [Detachment] is a supremely active deed which makes it possible to move unprejudiced and unafraid in to the center of evil, where one destroys what one really possesses and uses violence in the false presumption that life means power. The poor man can enter into this center with nonviolence because he has nothing to defend and he can destroy evil at its roots."[1]

Paul S. Minear: "...previous ideas about God, about the self, about such a community as the church, about the invisible realm out of which desires emerge and actions are born—all these ideas have to be radically revised. They begin to make sense in a world of thought where old words are being used to point to new relationships. Peace is one of those homespun words that can be used as a key to this new language and to life in this new world. In this new creation, peace refers primarily to the occasions when the divine takes over the control center of the individual heart and when the Father, in being worshiped, takes over the control center of his worshiping family. This peace is not a condition to be described simply in psychological terms, nor is it something whose effects can be measured simply in sociological terms. It comes, as the benedictions imply, when crucifixion-like events are transformed through Jesus Christ into resurrection-like fulfillments."[2]

LaFargue: "Even when people make up after a fight, hurt and hostile feelings remain. How can the cycle of hurting be broken? The person concerned about self-importance will always insist on her rights. The person secure in herself can afford to be generous all the time—careful of her responsibilities, but willing to overlook what others owe her. So she can be an agent of peace."[3]

PERFECTION/UNITY/WHOLENESS.

Lao Tzu: "There have been those of old who partook of the One;
Heaven partakes of the One,
And so becomes clear;
Earth partakes of the One,
And so it is at rest;
Spirits partake of the One,
And so are empowered;
The valley partakes of the One,
And so becomes full;
The Ten Thousand Things partake of the One,
And so flourish;
Dukes and kings partake of the One,
And so the world is stabilized—
They are what they are because of the One." (TTC, 39)

"But in integral self-cultivation, it is possible to achieve
a complete metamorphosis, to transcend your
emotional and biological limitations and evolve to
a higher state of being.
By staying out of the shadow and following this
simple path, you become extraordinary,
unfathomable, a being of profound cosmic subtlety.
You outlive time and space by realizing the subtle
truth of the universe." (HHC, 78)

Chuang Tzu: "Bright Dazzlement asked Nonexistence, 'Sir, do you exist or do you not exist?' Unable to obtain any answer, Bright Dazzlement stared intently at the other's face and form—all was vacuity and blankness. He stared all day but could see nothing, listened but could hear no sound, stretched out his hand but grasped nothing. 'Perfect!' exclaimed Bright Dazzlement. "Who can reach such perfection? I can conceive of the existence of nonexistence, but not of the nonexistence of nonexistence. Yet this man has reached the stage of the nonexistence of nonexistence. How could I ever reach such perfection!" (Chapter 22, "Knowledge Wandered North")

Jesus: "So be perfect, just as your heavenly Father is perfect." (Mt 5:48)

聖人不行而知 不見而名 不為而成

PERFECTION/UNITY/WHOLENESS.

Far from demanding the impossible absolute moral indefectability that was the Hellenic ideal, or requiring adherence to the religious-legalistic sense of fulfilling the entire code of cultic law, the biblical word (*tāmîm*) for perfection connotes the idea of wholeness: To be perfect is to serve God wholeheartedly, unreservedly and with complete attention.1 Byzantine spiritual writers, especially those of the Cappadocian School, contemplated perfection as a constant growth towards spiritual maturity; as Paul wrote: "I continue my pursuit in hope that I may possess it, since I have indeed been taken possession of by Christ [Jesus]" (Phil 3:12). The editor of the *Westminster Dictionary of Christian Spirituality* cites the Taoist-like phrasing of Methodist scholar W. F. Lofthouse on the subject: "Perfection is an attitude of the mind; and if so (as every saint and lover really knows), attainment and non-attainment imply each other; they are one and the same thing."2

Growth towards wholeness, towards spiritual maturity, has been spoken of in other contexts as "loving with the [divine and all-inclusive] Love with which we are loved."3 In this perspective, St. Isaac of Syria wrote the following: "The sign of having reached perfection is this: if a man were to be condemned ten times a day to be burned alive for loving his neighbor, and yet not be content with this, as was shown by Moses (Ex 32: 32), Paul (Rom 9:3) and other apostles. God surrendered His own Son to death on a cross, through love for His creatures. If He had something more precious to give, He would have given it to us, to make our race His own. Imitating Him, all the saints, in pursuit of perfection, strive to emulate God by the perfection of their love for their neighbor."4

St. Maximus the Confessor: "Listen to the words of those who have attained perfect love: 'Who shall separate us from the love of Christ? Shall tribulation, or distress, or persecution, or famine, or nakedness, or peril, or sword? As it is written, for thy sake we are killed all the day long; we are accounted as sheep for the slaughter. Nay in all these things we are more than conquerors through him that loved us. For I am persuaded, that neither death, nor life, nor angels, nor principalities, nor powers, nor things present, not things to come, nor height nor depth, nor any creature, shall be able to separate us from the love of God, which is in Christ Jesus our Lord.' (Rom 8:38–39)."5

Jennifer DeWeerth: "The Sermon on the Mount is quite serious about the call to perfection, in a way that has not always been recognized. By this I mean that the call to perfection is not just held out as a tantalizing chimera, a mirage that dissolves whenever we get near it, a brutal reminder that we cannot achieve righteousness but only sinfulness. No, the Sermon on the Mount believes in the real possibility of righteousness; it believes that such righteousness is the *telos* or perfect goal for us. For the Sermon on the Mount, human perfection is not impossible."

"...God has encouraged and reconciled us, and thereby we can love courageously. By God's righteousness, we are enabled to strive for righteousness, and in our context this means exercising justice informed by Christian faith. Indeed the church simply is where faith in God energizes a love that imitates God's love, energizes a righteousness that imitates God's righteousness, a perfection that imitates God's perfection. Be perfect as your God is perfect."[6]

The Taoist sense of "perfection" actually lies *beyond* the clearness, rest, empowerment, etc., mentioned in chapter 39 of the *Tao Te Ching* in that it *includes* their reversions to their opposite poles—the whole of which bespeaks the cyclical workings of the perfect Tao.

Fung Yu-lan describes the perfected one thusly: "He is absolutely happy, because he transcends the ordinary distinction of things. He also transcends the distinction between the self and the world, the 'me' and the 'non-me.' Therefore he has no self. His is one with the Tao."[7]

PRACTICAL VIRTUE.

Lao Tzu: "The best conduct leaves behind no trace;
The best speech is flawless;
The best calculation requires no counters;
The best door had neither bolt nor bar,
Yet cannot be opened;
The best knot requires neither rope nor twine,
and yet cannot be untied. (TTC, 27)

"Giving to others selflessly and anonymously, radiating
light throughout the world and illuminating your
own darknesses, your virtue becomes a refuge for
yourself and all being." (HHC, 47)

Jesus: "...take care not to perform righteous deeds in order that people may see them; otherwise, you will have no recompense from your heavenly Father. When you give alms, do not blow a trumpet before you, as the hypocrites do in the synagogues and in the streets to win the praise of others. Amen, I say to you, they have received their reward. But when you give alms, do not let your left hand know what your right hand is doing, so that your almsgiving may be secret. And your Father who sees in secret will repay you." (Mt 6: 1–4)

PRACTICAL VIRTUE.

Almsgiving was a cardinal act of righteousness in Jesus' religious culture—the word *tzedekah* meant both almsgiving and righteousness. *Hypokrites was* the Greek word for actor. The staging of one's display of righteousness for self-aggrandizement (i.e., to gain the admiration of others) is actually to give, in a manner of speaking, to the spiritually stunted self. To give humbly of the self in imitation of Christ is enriching to others: "For you know the gracious act of our Lord Jesus Christ, that for your sake he became poor although he was rich, so that by his poverty you might become rich." (2 Cor 8:9)

If "tracelessness" is identified either with perfection or lack of calculation (Ellen M. Chen) on one hand, or with being of ultimate and pure reality (Wing-Tsit Chan) on the other, then Jesus' recommended manner of dispensing charity is exemplary of perfect giving.

PRACTICAL WISDOM.

Lao Tzu: "A tree whose girth can fill a man's arms grows from a tiny shoot;
A nine-level terrace begins with a handful of earth;
A journey of one thousand *li* starts beneath one's feet." (TTC, 64)

Jesus: "Which one of you would hand his son a stone when he asks for a loaf of bread, or a snake when he asks for a fish?" (Mt 7:9)

"Let your 'Yes' mean 'Yes,' and your 'No' mean 'No.'" (Mt 5:37)

"Do people pick grapes from thornbushes, or figs from thistles?" (Mt 7:16)

"People do not put new wine into old wineskins. Otherwise the skins burst, the wine spills out, and the skins are ruined." (Mt 9:17)

"Where the body is, there also the vultures will gather." (Lk 17:37)

"If a blind person leads a blind person, both will fall into a pit." (Mt 15:14)

"Salt is good, but if salt itself loses its taste, with what can its flavor be restored? It is fit neither for the soil nor for the manure pile; it is thrown out. Whoever has ears to hear ought to hear." (Lk 14:34–35)

"...be shrewd as serpents and simple as doves." (Mt 10:16)

PRACTICAL WISDOM.

The simple and patently obvious verities of everyday life are often the most effective carriers of profound religious truths. Biblical wisdom literature is the product of the effort of ancient oriental peoples to gather, preserve and express, usually in aphoristic style, the results of human experience as an aid toward understanding and solving the problems of life. In Israel especially, the movement concerned itself with such basic and vital problems as humanity's origin and destiny, the quest for happiness, the problem of suffering, of good and evil in human conduct, of death, and the state beyond the grave. In times of personal and social crisis, what was honored as received wisdom assisted in the preservation of peace, unity and good will.[1] Throughout the first Christian centuries, the developing understanding of Jesus the Christ owes much to the doctrine of Jesus as personified Wisdom.[2]

Taoism's preference for the plain, simple, pure and genuine in thought, speech and action is evident in its ideal of the "uncarved block" (*p'u*). Lao Tzu admonished readers of the *Tao Te Ching* to "preserve simplicity, embrace the uncarved block" (chapter 19, "Mastering Life"). Chuang Tzu wrote, "In uncarved simplicity the people attain their true nature." (Chapter 9, "Horses' Hoofs")

"Chiao Hung [1541–1620] says, 'The ways of the world become daily more artificial. Hence we have names like wisdom and reason, kindness and justice, cleverness and profit. Those who understand the Tao see how artificial they are and how inappropriate they are to rule the world. They aren't as good as getting people to focus their attention on the undyed and the uncarved. By wearing the undyed and holding the uncarved, our self-interest and desires wane. The undyed and the uncarved refer to our original nature.'"[3]

"Ho-shang Kung [d. 159 B.C.?] says, 'Others seek the ornamental. The sage seeks the simple. Others seek form. The sage seeks Virtue.'"[4]

REPUDIATION OF POWER.

Chuang Tzu: "Once, when Chuang Tzu was fishing in the P'u river, the king of Ch'u sent two officials to go and announce to him: 'I would like to trouble you with the administration of my realm.'

"Chuang Tzu held on to the fishing pole and, without turning his head, said, 'I have heard that there is a sacred tortoise in Ch'u that has been dead for three thousand years. The king keeps it wrapped in cloth and boxed, and stores it in the ancestral temple. Now would this tortoise rather be dead and have its bones left behind and honored? Or would it rather be alive and dragging its tail in the mud?'

"'It would rather be alive and dragging its tail in the mud,' said the two officials.

"Chuang Tzu said, 'Go away! I'll drag my tail in the mud!'" (Chapter 17, "Autumn Floods")

"Then [the devil] took [Jesus] up and showed him all the kingdoms of the world in a single instant. The devil said to him, 'I shall give to you all this power and their glory; for it has been handed over to me, and I may give it to whomever I wish. All this will be yours, if you worship me.' Jesus said to him in reply, 'It is written:

"You shall worship the Lord, your God,
and him alone shall you serve."'" (Lk 4:5–8)

REPUDIATION OF POWER.

James W. Douglass: "Given the sense of the revolutionary milieu and of Jesus' own passion for justice, it is not difficult to feel the reality of this temptation that he take up the sword against imperial forces and attempt to seize all power for the people. But the prevailing argument in Jesus' mind against Satan's offer is, in Lukes's text, the very argument made by Satan himself....The power of these kingdoms, the power of the sword, belongs to Satan. To seize the sword and Caesar's power, for whatever end, is simply to worship Satan, and Jesus' reply is that God alone must be worshiped and served. For the sword of the world's kingdoms usurps the power of God, who alone has legitimate power over life and death."[1]

Chuang Tzu's story presumes a number of Taoist principles: Will to importance not only brings the person's own downfall; it also turns one away from the process of self-cultivation.[2] On the sheer practical level, self-effacement is more desirable than self-promotion; the one who is selfless and secure in him/herself can be free to be for others.[3]

REPUTATION.

Lao Tzu: "He who desires the admiration of the world will do
well to amass a great fortune and then give it away.
The world will respond with admiration in proportion
to the size of the treasure. Of course, this is meaningless.

"Stop striving for admiration. Place your esteem on the Tao. Live in
accord with it, share with others the teachings that lead to it, and you
will be immersed in the blessings that flow from it." (HHC, 9)

*Jesus: "Woe to you Pharisees! You love the seat of honor in synagogues
and greetings in marketplaces. Woe to you! You are like unseen graves
over which people unknowingly walk." (Lk 11: 43–44)*

*"You justify yourselves in the sight of others, but God knows your hearts;
for what is of human esteem is an abomination in the sight of God." (Lk
16:15)*

*"I do not accept human praise;...How can you believe, when you accept
praise from one another and do not seek the praise that comes from
the only God?" (Jn 5:41–44)*

REPUTATION.

Spiritual writer Isaias Powers does not shrink from naming overconcern for good repute as a root cause of sin: in imitation of the One who has come to serve, the kingdom requires service to others rather than praise from others.[1]

Holmes Welch elucidates from the Taoist perspective: "...favor can lead one to infatuation. Disgrace can lead him to seek revenge upon those who have disgraced him or in whose eyes he has been disgraced. Even favor can lead one to seek revenge, for it puts him in the position of being patronized. In either case, once he submits himself to the goads of public opinion, he will find it hard to keep his balance and even harder to continue the search for his original nature."[2]

RESPONSIBILITY FOR SELF.

Lao Tzu: "If one cultivates it (Tao) within one's self,
One's virtue becomes genuine;
If one cultivates it within one's own family,
One's virtue abounds;
If one cultivates it within one's community,
One's virtue endures;
If one cultivates it within one's country,
One's virtue flourishes;
If one cultivates it within the world,
One's virtue prevails.
Thus, see other selves through one's self;
See other families through one's family;
See other communities through one's community;
See other countries through one's country." (TTC, 54)

"Truly, the greatest gift you have to give is that of your
own self-transformation." (HHC, 75)

"The cleansing of spiritual contamination is not the responsibility of the
teacher, but of the student." (HHC, 73)

"Nonetheless, superior people can awaken during times of turmoil to
lead others out of the mire.
But how can one liberate the many?
By first liberating his own being.
He does this not by elevating himself, but by lowering himself.
He lowers himself to that which is simple and modest and truthful,
and by integrating it into himself,
he becomes a master of simplicity, modesty, truth." (HHC, 77)

*Jesus: "Neither do I condemn you. Go, [and] from now on do not sin
anymore." (Jn 8:11)*

The context of Jesus's words is the story of the woman about to be stoned for the sin of adultery. Jesus challenges those about to administer religious justice to first confront the flawed narratives of their own lives. The stones fall from their hands. In his bid, "Go, and sin no more," Jesus offers the woman—and each believer—the possibility of liberation from a self-limiting past.

Scott Peck offers the following commentary on Jesus' parable of the wise awaiting maidservants who did not share their lamp oil with the foolish maid-servants who had none (Mt 25:1–13): "The parable struck me as totally un-Christian. What on earth is Christianity about if it isn't about sharing?...It didn't take me long to realize that the oil in this parable was a symbol of preparation, and that what Jesus was saying to us—realist that He was—was that we cannot share our preparation. You cannot do others' homework for them. Or if you did their homework, you cannot earn their degree for them, which is the symbol of preparation. So we cannot give away our preparation. The only thing we can do—and it is often very difficult—is to try as best we can to impart to others a motive for them to prepare themselves."[1]

Ku-ying Ch'en: "Lao Tzu suggests that the process of establishing the Tao in the world must begin with a nurturing of it in the individual. This is consistent with the idea that a true understanding of the Tao should be sought in the examination of man's natural endowment—it should be sought 'inwardly' rather than 'externally.' Nurturing the Tao in the individual is the fundamental step in realizing one's natural potential and in understanding the proper method of governing others. As Chuang Tzu states, 'The genuine substance of the Tao is used to govern oneself; its trimmings and superfluity, are used to govern the nation and its families ("Jang Wang"). That which Chuang Tzu refers to as governing 'the nation and its families' is the natural sequel or extension of fulfilling oneself. In the passage which discusses 'a scrutinizing of oneself' and ultimately 'a scruti-nizing of one's own world,' the point which Lao Tzu stresses is that the individual must understand the internal before he can grasp the principles of the external."[2]

From *The Book of Balance and Harmony,*: "To promote worthy qualities and accomplish works, nothing is more important than correcting oneself. Once the self is correct, everything is correct. Forms and names cannot stand but for correctness, tasks cannot succeed but for correctness.

"All activities start from oneself. Therefore developmental work requires self-correction as a foundation. When one deals with people after having corrected oneself, then people too will become correct. When one manages affairs after having corrected oneself, affairs too become correct. When one responds to things after having corrected oneself, things too become correct.

"Only a unified correctness in the world is able to master the myriad changes in the world. So we know that correcting oneself is the great function of developmental work, and the stairway to sagehood."[3]

SEEKING/FINDING.

Lao Tzu: "[With Tao] one seeks and obtains." (TTC, 62)

Jesus: "Ask and it will be given to you;
seek and you will find;
knock and the door will be opened to you.
For everyone who asks, receives;
and the one who seeks, finds;
and to the one who knocks,
the door will be opened." (Mt 7:7–8)

SEEKING/FINDING.

Ask, seek, find: scripture scholars teach that the verbs, in context, refer to prayer. With regard to the nature of praying itself, it could be suggested that what Jesus is recommending here is capitalizing more on the faithfulness of the prayed-to than the pray-er. In any case, the close covenant relationship between God and devotee is solidified in the experience of prayer. How does one sense that the pray-er is being sought out by the prayed-to? Spiritual writer Joyce Rupp suggests taking counsel from the following set of intuited indicators within one's "inner life": restlessness within or an unnamed loneliness; a hunger for deep bonding; questions that keep surfacing; sudden awareness or clearer vision about life's meaning; an unexpected sense of deep contentment or peace; darkness that has the aura of mystery or searching; a desire for greater truth; a hopefulness that rises in one's spirit; a yearning for justice; an overwhelming awareness of God's mercy; a bonding with beauty. Conversely, responses to the question, How do we know when we are seeking God out? include the following: willingness to sit with the unnamed stirrings within; the discipline of reflecting, pondering, meditating; confrontation of fears, anxieties and concerns; deliberate decisions to go deeper; owning and claiming one's inherent goodness; savoring the entrance into situations that involve risk and struggle; actively bonding with a community or others who seek God; welcoming the goodness in others.[1]

In the tradition of St. Augustine, the searching and finding is ultimately a process of coalescence involving the subject and object: to seek God is to find one's true self, and to seek one's true self is to find God. (*Confessions,* 5.22)

In Taoism, seeking-as-prayer is replaced by seeking-as-preparation. Chuang Tzu: "Nieh Ch'ueh asked P'i-i about the Way, P'i-i said, 'Straighten up your body, unify your vision, and the harmony of Heaven will come to you. Call in your knowledge, unify your bearing, and the spirits will come to dwell with you. Virtue will be your beauty, the Way will be your home....'" (Chapter 22, "Knowledge Wandered North")

SELF AS NO-THING.

Chuang Tzu: "Tzu-Ch'i of South Wall sat leaning on his armrest, staring up at the sky and breathing—vacant and far away, as though he'd lost his companion. Yen Ch'eng Tzu-yu, who was standing by his side in attendance, said, 'What is this? Can you really make the body like a withered tree and the mind like dead ashes? The man leaning on the armrest now is not the one who leaned on it before!'

"Tzu-ch'i said, 'You do well to ask the question, Yen. Now I have lost myself. Do you understand that? You hear the piping of men, but haven't heard the piping of earth. Or if you've heard the piping of earth, you haven't heard the piping of Heaven!'" (Chapter 2, "Discussion on Making All Things Equal")

Jesus: "...whoever loses his life for my sake will save it."
(Lk 9:24)

SELF AS NO-THING.

Teilhard de Chardin's description of his spiritual journey into himself is now classic:

"I took the lamp and, leaving the zone of everyday occupations and relationships where everything is clear, I went down into my inmost self, to the deep abyss whence I feel dimly that my power emanates. But as I moved further and further away from my conventional certainties by which social life is superficially illuminated, I became aware that I was losing contact with myself. At each step of the descent, a new person was disclosed within me of whose name I was no longer sure and who no longer obeyed me. And when I had to stop my exploration because the path faded from beneath my steps, I found a bottomless abyss at my feet, and out of it—arising I knew not from where—the current which I dare call *my* life....In the last resort the profound, like the newborn life, escape our grasp entirely."[1]

Joseph Powers' analysis is worthy of being presented at length: "It is extremely difficult to speak of this experience. Those who know most about it, mystical or Zen masters, resort to poetry, aphorism, paradox—anything to break down the human propensity for objectification and security...John of the Cross's succession of *ni eso* [not this]...*ni eso...ni eso*...is not simply a matter of theoretical or abstract options among which one makes choices. Rather, it is a matter of successive and deeper perceptions of the very reality of one's own personal identity, realities which, in the last analysis, must all be rejected. It is a process of the loss of 'empirical ego,' the very identifiability of one's self as a person....

"Perhaps the most suitable name for the experience of total self-transcendence is 'the experience of no-thing-ness.' What this means is that one transcends thing after thing as the center of one's consciousness and identity. It becomes *experientially* clear that one exists literally *ex nihilo*—out of no thing. No particular or series of personal achievements, no person or community, no conscious or unconscious goals or personal forces—no *thing* is one's personal core. There is only, in Teihard's words, an 'abyss.' It is, in Merton's words, 'kenotic transformation, an emptying of all the contents of the ego-consciousness to become a void...' R. N. Bellah speaks of it in terms of losing one's 'home.' Perhaps the best description is in the pungent aphorism of Norman O. Brown, 'I'm thousands, I'm an in-divide-you-all, I'm no un (i.e., nun, no-un, no one).' A long tradition refers to it as the final stage of 'mortification,' a 'death to self.'"[2]

E. M. Chen: "In Taoism, negation is the very nature of the absolute. Tao alone is the absolute nothingness that penetrates all beings. Beings are able to penetrate other beings only to the extent that they approximated nothing or contain in themselves some degree of nothing. The account of the successful butcher in the *Chuang Tzu,* chapter 3, illustrates the Taoist concept of freedom: 'When I first began to cut up a bullock, I saw only the bullock. Now I meet the bullock with my spiritual (*shen*), not physical, eye. Senses only know immobility but spirit follows the movement. Conforming to nature's (*t'ien,* heaven) own reasoning my knife slices through the great crevices and glides through the great cavities, moving along [the bullock's] own structure, avoiding tendons and particularly the great bones....Now at the joints [of the bones and tendons] there are interstices. Yet the edge of my chopper [is so sharp that it] has not thickness. To insert what has no thickness into what has crevices (*wu hou ju yu chien*), certainly there is plenty of room to move about.'"[3]

Jesus, coming to nothing in the supreme sacrifice of self upon the cross, becomes so boundless as to be able to "descend into hell" and extend the boundaries of his victory over death, even there.

天長地久，天地所以能長久者，
以其不自生，故能長生。
是故聖人後其身而身先，
外其身而身存。
非以其無私邪，
故能成
其私。

平彭子
堯章

SELFLESSNESS.

Lao Tzu: "Is it not just because one remains self-less
That one can sustain one's [true] self?" (TTC, 7)

"Practicing kindness and selflessness, you naturally
align your life with the Integral Way.
Aligning your life with the Integral Way, you begin
to eliminate the illusory boundaries between people
and societies, between darkness and light, between
life and death.
Eliminating these illusions, you gain the company of
the highest spiritual beings.
In their company, you are protected from negative
influences and your life energy cannot be dissolved.
Thus do you achieve immortality." (HHC, 36)

Jesus: "This is how you are to pray:
'Our Father in heaven,
hallowed be your name,
your kingdom come,
your will be done,
on earth as in heaven.'" (Mt 6:9–10)

SELFLESSNESS.

Jerome Kodell, O.S.B.: "The Pauline school reflects the insights of the apostle on self-denial. 'You were buried with him in baptism' (Col 2:12). 'If we have died with him we shall also live with him' (2 Tim 2:11)....Jesus handed himself over to us as a 'sacrificial offering' (Eph 5:2); we imitate his sacrificial spirit by living as children of the light, trying to learn 'what is pleasing to the Lord,' not to ourselves (Eph 5:10)."[1]

In the philosophy of Taoism, one of the problem-causing factors in human life is the self, or, more correctly, the living of life centered on the self. The self-centered life is the primary cause of ethical evil and narrowness of mindset; the remedy for both is the substitution of Tao-centeredness for self-centeredness.

Thomas Cleary: "To be 'oblivious of body and soul' means to entertain no image of person; to 'forget oneself' means to entertain no image of ego.
   "The pipes of heaven, earth, and humanity represent differences in the states of beings; the wind playing the pipes represents the underlying unity of the vital energy of life. Taoists try to become aware of this and harmonize with it.
   "The Taoist master Fu-kuei-tzu says, 'Humans are the most intelligent of beings, yet they change their attitudes in various unequal ways, because the real director is not present. If people would get the sense of the real director, then they would not be guided by the subjective psyche, but would spontaneously be on the Way.'"[2]

Liu I-ming: "The life of human beings is dependent on the three treasures of vitality, energy, and spirit; when the three treasures are together, people live, and when the three treasures are scattered, people die. If you want to get the three treasures together, first you must be selfless. When selfless, the mind is open; when the mind is open, the three treasures do not leak away or dissipate. There is only increase, there cannot be decrease."[3]

SOLICITUDE.

Lao Tzu : "Vast and boundless is Heaven's net [Tao],
Its mesh large and loose,
Yet misses nothing." (TTC, 73)

"Its virtue fosters them:
Rears them, nurtures them, harbors them,
Comforts them, feeds them, shelters them.
[Tao] gives them life, and yet is not possessive of them;
Benefits them, and yet expects no gratitude;
Rears them, and yet does not claim mastery over them.
This is called 'profoundly dark virtue.'" (TTC, 51)

*Jesus: "Are not two sparrows sold for a small coin? Yet not one of them
falls to the ground without your Father's knowledge. Even all the hairs of
your head are counted. So do not be afraid...." (Mt 10:29–30)*

SOLICITUDE.

By these words Jesus distills the notions of God as creator, knower, lover, protector and One who wills the salvation of His people. Although the term "providence" is not itself biblical, the idea of a wise, loving and powerful God who is everywhere at work in the world pervades the entire Bible. It is found in the story of creation and it underlies the whole history of Israel, from the call and election of Abraham and his offspring, through the events of the Exodus and the granting of the Covenant, the establishment of the monarch, to the Babylonian exile and the return. In the teaching of Jesus, God is Father who cares for us, answers our prayers (Lk 11:9–13), forgives us our sins as we forgive others (Mt 6:14–15), asks us (Mt 10:29–31) to live as His children (Mt 5:16), and calls us to the eternal life of the kingdom (Jn 6:40). The greatest expression of God's care is the sending of his Son as our redeemer.[1]

"Li Hsi-chai says, 'What the Way and Virtue bestow, they bestow without thought. No one orders them. It is simply their nature. It is their nature to beget and their nature to keep. It is their nature to cultivate and train, to steady and adjust, to nurture and protect. And because it is their nature, they never tire of begetting or expect a reward for what they give. This is what is meant by 'Dark Virtue.'"[2]

131

SOLITUDE/INWARDNESS.

Lao Tzu: "One can know the world without going out-of-doors;
One can see the Tao of Heaven without window-peeping." (TTC, 47)

Chuang Tzu: "The Heavenly is on the inside, the human is on the out-side." (Chapter 17, "Autumn Floods")

Jesus: "But when you pray, go to your inner room, close the door, and pray to your Father in secret. And your Father who sees in secret will repay you." (Mt 6:6)

SOLITUDE/INWARDNESS.

Psychologically and spiritually, solitude serves as the silent matrix for self-reflection and the essential condition for the fostering of intimacy with God and others.[1] Jesus is portrayed in the gospels both as a public figure and a seeker of solitude. Secluded mountain tops and outlying deserts were places to establish communion with the Father or to be personally tested; in either case, it was in solitude that he acquired the solace and the fortitude needed to continue his public ministry. He enjoined his disciples to do likewise (Mk 6:31). Throughout Christian history, countless others have likewise responded to the invitation.

John of the Cross considered desire for solitude as a mark of progress in a developing spiritual life: "The third and surest sign is that the soul takes pleasure in being alone, and waits with loving attentiveness upon God, without making any particular meditation, in inward peace and quietness and rest, without acts and exercises of the faculties—memory, understanding and will—at least without discursive acts, that is, without passing from one thing to another; the soul is alone, with an attentiveness and a knowledge, general and loving, as we said, but without any particular understanding and adverting not to what it is contemplating."[2]

Parker J. Palmer writes eloquently in the contemporary context on the spiritual benefits of solitude:
"Solitude eventually offers a quiet gift of grace, a gift that comes whenever we are able to face ourselves honestly: the gift of acceptance, of compassion, for who we are, as we are....It creates a space in which we can let go of our self-delusions and allow ourselves to be transformed by truth. As we do, we are better able to create a space to receive the world as it is, a space in which obedience in truth is practiced...we can feel the whole world's connections."[3]

Yi Wu comments that the intelligent one who knows the inner dynamics, rules, and essence of objects thereby knows, by extension, of the changes and development of all things in the world outside of one's immediate locality.[4]

The annals of Taoist poetry are replete with odes to solitude and inwardness. John Blofield provides a number of examples, this among them from Li T'ai-po:

"You ask me why I dwell
Amidst these jade-green hills?

I smile. No words can tell
The stillness in my heart.
The peach-bloom on the water,
How enchanting it drifts!
I live in another realm here
Beyond the world of men."

And from Ch'uan Te-yu:

"Dismounting from my horse,
Dusk falling on the wild,
I hear amidst the silence
The splash of mountain rill.
Birds sing and petals fall;
Of men there is not a trace.
The window of my hut
Is curtained with white cloud."[5]

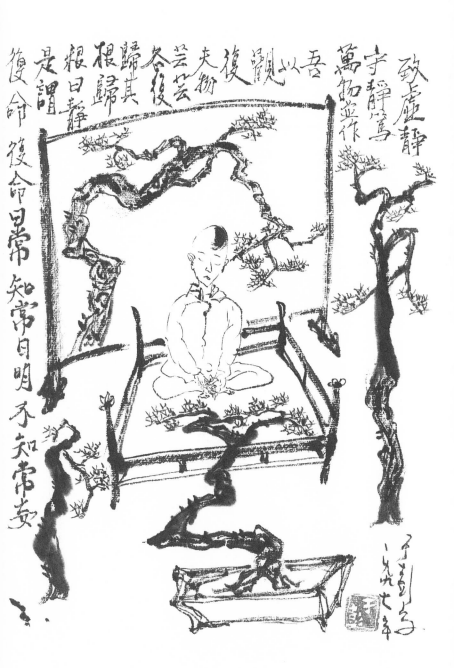

致虛極 守靜篤 萬物並作 吾以觀復 夫物芸芸 各復歸其根 歸根曰靜 是謂復命 復命曰常 知常曰明 不知常妄

一九七年

STILLNESS/REST/TRANQUILITY.

Lao Tzu: "Preserve tranquility to the utmost." (TTC, 16)

Jesus: "Come to me, all you who labor and are burdened, and I will give you rest." (Mt 11:28)

"Come away by yourselves to a deserted place and rest a while." (Mk 6:31)

STILLNESS/REST/TRANQUILITY.

In Christian scriptures, "rest" is a theological category describing salvation. In the New Testament, redemption is understood as the new exodus, both in the experience of Jesus himself (Lk 9:31) and in that of his followers (1 Cor 10:1–4). The rest into which Israel was to enter was only a foreshadowing of the rest to which Christians are called. The symbol of rest is explored in its deeper dimensions by the author of Hebrews, chapter 4, verses 1–11: because the promised land was the place of rest that God provided for his people, it was a share in his own rest, which he enjoyed after he had finished creating the world. The Greek form of the name Joshua, who led Israel in to the promised land, is Jesus (verse 8). The author of Hebrews plays upon the name but stresses the superiority of Jesus, who leads his followers into heavenly rest.[1]

For St. Antony the Great, physical rest is a privileged time in the spiritual life: "When you lie down on your bed, remember with thanksgiving the blessings and providence of God. Thereupon, filled with good thought, you will rejoice in spirit and the sleep of your body will mean sobriety of the soul; the closing of your eyes—a true knowledge of God, and your silence, brimming with the feeling of good, will wholeheartedly and with all its strength glorify the Almighty God, giving Him from the heart praises that rise on high."[2]

"Su Ch'e [1039–1112] says, 'We know how to act but not how to rest. We know how to talk but not how to keep still. We know how to remember but not how to forget. Everything we do leads to death. The sage dwells where there is neither life nor death.'"[3]

Kuan-yin [sixth century B.C.]: "As for the stillness of the sage, it is not that he is still because he says 'It is good to be still;' he is still because nothing among the myriad things is sufficient to disturb his heart. When water is still its clarity shows up the hairs of beard and eyebrows, its evenness coincides with the water level—the greatest carpenter takes his standard from it. If mere water clarifies when it is still, how much more the stillness of the quintessential and daemonic, the heart of the sage! He is the reflector of heaven and earth, the mirror of the myriad of things.
   "Emptiness, stillness, calm, serenity, Doing Nothing, are the even level of heaven and earth, the utmost reach of the Way and the Power; therefore the emperor, king, sage, comes to rest in them. At rest he empties, in emptiness is

filled; and what fills him sorts itself out. In emptying he is still, in stillness he is moved; and when he moves he succeeds."[4]

John Blofeld: "'The recluse's heart is a placid lake unruffled by the winds of circumstance.' I remember seeing these words inscribed above the doorway of one of the first Taoist hermitages I visited. Later I was to encounter words to the same effect carved upon rock, brushed on wall scrolls, spoken by Taoist masters and included in almost every book connected directly or indirectly with cultivation of the Way. If any one word is pre-eminent among Taoists, it is 'stillness.' One had only to inquire about the Way to be sure of some such answer as: 'To return to your original state of being, you must become a master of stillness. Activity for health's sake, never carried to the point of strain, must alternate with perfect stillness. Sitting motionless as a rock, turn next to stillness of mind. Close the gates of the senses. Fix your mind upon one subject or, even better, enter a state of objectless awareness. Turn the mind in upon itself and contemplate the inner radiance.'"[5]

五色令人目盲
五音令人耳聾
五味令人口爽
馳騁畋獵
令人心發狂
難得之貨令人行妨
是以聖人為腹
不為目
故去彼
取此

STORYTELLING.

Lao Tzu: "The inferior person, hearing of Tao, laughs heartily at it. If one did not laugh at it, it would not be Tao." (TTC, 41)

Jesus: "This is why I speak to them in parables, because 'they look but do not see and hear but do not listen or understand.' Isaiah's prophecy is fulfilled in them, which says:

> *'You shall indeed hear but not understand,*
> *you shall indeed look but never see.*
> *Gross is the heart of this people,*
> *they will hardly hear with their ears,*
> *they have closed their eyes,*
> *lest they see with their eyes*
> *and hear with their ears*
> *and understand with their heart and be converted*
> *and I heal them.'" (Mt 13:13–15)*

STORYTELLING.

"Christ is like a Zen master, constantly exploding illusions," writes Richard Rohr, O.F.M.[1] How so? Jesus described kingdom-appropriate values and attitudes in stories of the particular type known as "parables." Parables can be understood as "word-events" in that the kingdom and its effects—for example, joy and peace—become felt realities in those disposed to forsake former illusory understandings of self, world and God for the new understandings conveyed in the stories. That the medium (parable) is the message (kingdom) is never truer than when applied to parables appropriately responded to.

Robert Allinson argues that Chuang Tzu's intention is not to bring a change in conceptualization, but to effect a disengagement of conceptual and analytical powers in the reader altogether so that Tao may be apprehended.[2]

SUSTENANCE.

Lao Tzu: "Prize not rare goods, so that the people will not steal;
Display not objects of desire, so that the minds[a] of people will not become confused.
Accordingly, the Sage rules by emptying the minds of the people, and filling their stomachs,
Weakening their ambitions,
And strengthening their bones." (TTC, 3)

"[The wise one] eats the understanding that the named was born from the unnamed, that all being flows from nonbeing, that the describable world emanates from an indescribable source. He finds this subtle truth inside his own self, and becomes completely content." (HHC, 38)

Jesus: "Can you make the wedding guests fast while the bridegroom is with them?" (Lk 5: 34)

"It is written:

> *'One does not live by bread alone,*
> *but by every word that comes forth*
> *from the mouth of God.'" (Mt 4:4)*

---

[a] The Chinese character '*hsin*' generally means both 'mind' and 'heart,' avoiding the Western tendency to distinguish between intellectual and emotional centers while affirming a natural integration. Depending on the context, it can refer exclusively to either mind (intellect or reason) or the heart (emotions or feelings).—Translators.

SUSTENANCE.

E. M. Chen: "The *Tao Te Ching* is not against life's simple pleasures and teaches no asceticism....Like music that nourishes the soul and good food that nour-ishes the body, Tao is a nurturing principle at whose table all passers-by stop to feed. Although Tao is flavorless, invisible, and inaudible, it is an inexhaustible fountain dispensing safety, peace and contentment."[1]

Luke's use of the Hebrew Bible's bridegroom image for Jesus conveys the loving fidelity of God for God's people that is cause for celebratory joy and feasting.

In commenting on Jesus's response to being tempted to turn stone into bread, William Barclay provides a traditional interpretation regarding the true cause of human hunger and the nature of true sustenance: "It would have been to remove the symptoms without dealing with the disease. Men are hungry. But the question is, why are they hungry? Is it because of their own foolishness, and their own shiftlessness, and their own carelessness? Is it because there are some who selfishly possess too much while others possess too little? The real way to cure hunger is to remove the causes—and these causes are in men's souls. And above all there is a hunger of the heart which is not in material things to satisfy."[2]

THE TAUGHT.

Lao Tzu: "One who has established a firm foundation [Tao],
will not have it uprooted; One who embraces [Tao],
will not withdraw from it." (TTC, 54)

"Humbly respect and serve your teacher, and dedicate
your entire being unwaveringly to self-cultivation.
Then you will surely achieve self-mastery and be able
to help others in doing the same." (HHC, 80)

"So find a teacher who is an integral being,
a beacon who extends his light and virtue with equal ease to those who
appreciate him and those who don't.
Shape yourself in his mold, bathe in his nourishing radiance,
and reflect it out to the rest of the world.
You will come to understand an eternal truth:
there is always a peaceful home for a virtuous being." (HHC, 75).

*Jesus: "Everyone who listens to these words of mine and acts on them
will be like a wise man who built his house on rock. The rain fell, the
floods came, and the winds blew and buffeted the house. But it did not
collapse; it had been set solidly on rock. And everyone who listens to
these words of mine but does not act on them will be like a fool who built
his house on sand. The rain fell, the floods came, and the winds blew and
buffeted the house. And it collapsed and was completely ruined." (Mt 7:
24-27)*

THE TAUGHT.

Both growth and development in the created realm involve risk-taking, yet to constantly abide in a state of uncertainty and potential peril (that is, to be under constant threat to one's physical, psychological, or spiritual well-being) without the surety of safe recourse makes that same growth and development an impossibility. "To hold to nothing is to fall for everything," states the familiar adage. As founder, foundation and minister of the restored relationship between God and his people (cf. Heb 7:22), Jesus is the guarantee of its eternal permanence.

"Wu Ch'eng [1249–1333] says, 'Those who plant it right, plant without planting. Thus it is never uprooted. Those who hold it right, hold without holding. Thus it is never ripped away.'"[1]

"Wang An-Shih [1021–1086] says, "What we plant right is virtue. What we hold right is oneness. When virtue flourishes, distant generations give praise."[2]

Yi Wu: "If things are held by your hand, external strength can pull it away. So if the real holder holds things in the heart, it unites one which is chi (Tao), and will never separate."[3]

THE TEACHER (I).

Lao Tzu: "I alone am nebulous and in the dark—
tranquil as the sea,
Gliding, as if without purpose!" (TTC, 20)

Jesus: "Foxes have dens and birds of the sky have nests, but the Son of Man has nowhere to rest his head." (Mt 8:20)

"The wind blows where it wills, and you can hear the sound it makes, but you do not know where it comes from or where it goes; so it is with everyone who is born of the Spirit." (Jn 3:8)

THE TEACHER (I).

The Messiah entered a world that knew him not (Jn 1:10); his own birth was depicted by the evangelist Luke as occurring in circumstances devoid of comfort and security; he was well aware of the degree to which his word and person were being rejected by those occupying the precincts of established places of thought and worship. Yet, as the one whose self-identity was as "the Way" (Jn 14:6), there is no location in creation that could be considered as being "out of the way" for himself or those who share his life as long as he is present there. Itineracy is not possible for anyone for whom every place is home.

Taoism emphasizes the inner, psychological freedom of the Taoist sage who is free to "come and go without any attachments."[1]

THE TEACHER (II).

Lao Tzu: "Unattached to her accomplishments, taking credit for nothing
at all, she guides the whole world by
guiding the individuals who come to her.
She shares her divine energy with her students,
encouraging them, creating trials to strengthen them,
scolding them to awaken them,
directing the stream of their lives
toward the infinite ocean of the Tao." (HHC, 80)

"[The Sage] claims nothing;
Gives them life and yet does not possess them;
Succors them and yet does not appropriate them;
the task is accomplished,
and yet [the Sage] claims no credit.
Only because [the Sage] claims no credit,
It is not taken away." (TTC, 2)

*Jesus: "Jerusalem, Jerusalem, you who kill the prophets and stone those
sent to you, how many times I yearned to gather your children together
as a hen gathers her brood under her wings...." (Lk 13:34)*

*"Just so, the Son of Man did not come to be served but to serve and to
give his life as a ransom for many." (Mt 20:28)*

THE TEACHER (II).

Teacher, sage, counselor, master, preceptor, pedagogue; the exact title is of no consequence. One who possesses such authority as to merit being so addressed is one who acts not for the self but for others. As teacher, as love, Jesus the Christ is that which is "taught." Thomas Merton explored the meaning of this profound identity: "The power of the sage is then the very power which has been revealed in the gospels as Pure Love. *Deus caritas est* (God is love) is the full manifestation of the truth hidden in the nameless Tao, and yet still leaves Tao nameless. For love is not a name, any more than Tao is. One must go beyond the word and enter into communion with the reality before he can know anything about it."[1]

THE TEACHINGS.

Lao Tzu: "My words are very easy to understand, and very easy to practice." (TTC, 70)

"Accordingly, the Sage is four-square without piercing;
Sharp-cornered, and yet not harmful;
Upright, and yet not self-righteous;
Luminous, and yet not blinding." (TTC, 58)

*Jesus: "Take my yoke upon you and learn from me, for I am meek and
humble of heart; and you will find rest for yourselves. For my yoke is
easy, and my burden light." (Mt 11:29–30)*

THE TEACHINGS.

The teachers of Jesus' time taught that God created a highly structured and ordered world and that religious laws, commandments, prescriptions and prohibitions provided the blueprint of that order. To recognize and obey the authority of biblical law in every detail of daily living (metaphorically, to take upon oneself the "yoke" of the law) was to align oneself with the cosmic and social order of God's design. The commandments of Jesus are quantitatively easier because they are less in number and concentrated on the essentials—love of God and of neighbor. Even though his commandments are qualitatively more difficult (e.g., his parable of the Good Samaritan implies that the category of "enemy" is included in that of "neighbor"), the assistance and consolation of the (new) lawgiver is always assured.

LaFargue: "The Tao that we teach: It's nothing strikingly unusual. It is found in the middle of ordinariness..."[1]

Chung-yuan Chang: "According to Taoists, one lets one's ego-self go through reduction or laying down one's load. Therefore, Lao Tzu says that his teaching is easy to follow. To lay down one's load is to reach the source of all creativity and potentiality."[2]

"Wang P'ang [1044–1076] says, 'Because the sage teaches us to be in harmony with the source of our life, his words are simple, and his deeds are ordinary. Those who look within themselves understand. Those who follow their own nature do what is right. Difficulties arise when we turn away from the trunk and follow the branches.'"[3]

"Yen Tsun [fl. 53–24 B.C.] says, 'Wild geese fly for days but don't know what exists beyond the sky. Officials and scholars work for years, but none of them knows the extent of the Way. It's beyond the ken and beyond the reach of narrow-minded, one-sided people.'"[4]

E. M. Chen: "The message here is that the Way is easy to know and easy to practice.... The deepest truth is also the plainest and easiest to know and to carry out, since it is present everywhere. Yet people have so lost touch with the primal truth that they can no longer comprehend or practice it. As a result they look for solutions in the hard and difficult."[5]

151

Yi Wu: "Taoist thinking inherits the spirit of Chinese philosophy with emphasis on life praxis. The Sage will use observations from the seasons and atmospheric phenomena as an example to teach so that normal people can easily feel it and it is easy to understand. If people learn the way of the earth, if they plant then they will reap, then all will be able to follow and carry through."[6]

持而盈之不如其已揣而梲之　不可長保

金玉滿堂莫之能守

富貴而驕自遺其咎功成身退天之道

平龍

九九七年

THE THREAT OF UNCHECKED DESIRES.

Lao Tzu: "The Sage desires no-desire,
Prizes not rare goods, learns to un-learn,
Redeems the errors of the masses,[a]
In order to assist the natural spontaneity
Of the Ten Thousand Things without daring to act [in excess]." (TTC, 64)

"If, in transforming themselves, their desire is activated,
I shall restrain it with the Uncarved Block of no-name." (TTC, 37)

Jesus: "The seed sown among thorns is the one who hears the word, but then worldly anxiety and the lure of riches choke the word and it bears no fruit." (Mt 13:22)

---

[a] Most translators render the character '*fu*' as 'to return' or 'to restore,' and the character '*kuo*' as 'to miss' or 'to lose.' However, since in this context '*kuo*' indicates mistakes or errors, '*fu*' should be read as 'to redeem' or 'to compensate.'—Translators.

THE THREAT OF UNCHECKED DESIRES.

As a traditional term in Christian spiritual literature, "passions" are those alien, irrational, excessive and unbridled appetites that, when willingly entertained by the exercise of free choice, disrupt one's natural disposition towards godliness. To attain to the spiritual ideal of "dispassion" is—with the assistance of God's grace—to reacquire the disposition in which the desires are again assembled, integrated and ordered toward what is good and godlike. God is restored as the true end of human yearning; one is again living in accord with the foundational meaning and "logic" of human existence.[1] As in Taoism, dispassion is not to be construed as dull insensibility.

"No-desire" in Taoism is not only the absence of the wantonness that blocks the simple and natural flow of Tao; it is also a principle whose application extends to the very thought of attaining any spiritual achievement whatsoever: "Ch'eng Hsuan-ying [fl. 647–663] says, 'When people first change and begin to cultivate the Tao, they think about reaching a goal. Once this desire arises, it must be stilled with the Tao's nameless simplicity.'"[2]

UNITY OF FOCUS.

Lao Tzu: "To know harmony is to be in accord with the eternal (Tao)."
(TTC, 55)

"Seek instead to keep your mind undivided.
Dissolve all ideas into the Tao." (HHC, 41)

"Don't go crazy with the worship of idols, images, and ideas;
this is like putting a new head on top of the
head you already have." (HHC, 45)

"Don't analyze the Tao.
Strive instead to live it:
silently, undividedly, with your whole harmonious being." (HHC, 30)

*Jesus: "Every kingdom divided against itself will be laid waste, and no
town or house divided against itself will stand." (Mt 12:25)*

"No servant can serve two masters." (Lk 16:13)

UNITY OF FOCUS.

Thomas Merton speaks of dividedness in mind or will in terms of "impure intentionality." In such a state, one is plunged into a confusion of doubtful choices and the welter of multiple possibilities. Since one is caught between two conflicting wills—God's and one's own—simple and clear decision-making becomes an impossibility, as do personal happiness and peace. The one of conflicted and divided mind or will has twice as much to think about as one who seeks only God's will or mind. Inner freedom is lost. Only those possessing focused, pure intentions can be clear sighted and prudent.[1]

"Te-ch'ing [1546–1623] says, 'Those who cultivate the Tao should first focus their minds. When the mind doesn't stray, it becomes calm. When the mind becomes calm, breath becomes balanced. When breath becomes balanced, essence becomes stable, spirit becomes serene, and our true nature is restored. Once we know how to breathe, we know how to endure. And once we know how to endure, we know our true nature. If we don't know our true nature but only know how to nourish our body and lengthen our lives, we end up harming our body and destroying our lives. A restless mind disturbs the breath. When the breath is disturbed, the essence weakens. And when the essence weakens, the body withers.'"[2]

THE UNITY OF OPPOSITES.

Lao Tzu: "Being and Non-Being give birth to each other.
Difficult and easy complement each other;
Long and short balance each other;
High and low incline toward each other;
[Cosmic] sound and [human] voice harmonize with each other;
Front and back follow each other.
Accordingly, the Sage handles human affairs with no-effort,
Practices the teaching of no-words." (TTC, 2)

Jesus: "You belong to what is below, I belong to what is above." (Jn 8:23)

UNITY OF OPPOSITES.

In the Augustinian reading of salvation history, the manifestation of human "lowness"—because it occasioned the divine redemptive condescension from "above"—is expressed by a term that is itself an unexpected union of opposites: *felix culpa* (happy fault).

In commenting on the Gospel of John, Catholic theologian Edward Schillebeeckx writes: "We constantly find contrasts like 'from below'–'from above', light-darkness, truth-lie, life-God, God–'the prince of this world'. And these positive or negative qualifications are interchangeable within their category. However, it is striking that all these contrasts relate to the acceptance or the rejection of Jesus....Here there is an existential dualism, really a form of the monism of grace."[1]

Within this thought-form of "union of opposites" is the popular prayer of St. Francis of Assisi ("...for it is in giving that we receive, it is in pardoning that we are pardoned, and it is in dying that we are born to eternal life.")

Chung-yuan Chang: "Chinese logicians see the truth of the unity or syntheses of opposites. Thus, they say: 'I go to Yueh today, but I arrived there yesterday.'"[2]

Kristofer Shipper comments on the sense of paradox that is inherent in so many of the Taoist expressions of united oppositions: "The constant use of paradoxes is indeed primarily intended to detach us from any general idea or prejudice. But one may well ask whether these paradoxes do not have a higher meaning which reaches beyond rhetoric and continually refers to another dimension, to something passing our common knowledge and our normal ideas."[3]

VACUOUS SUPERFICIALITY.

Lao Tzu: "Nowadays, [people] are courageous, but lack parental care;
Are expansive, but lack frugality;
Assert themselves, without putting themselves behind.
[The doom of] death!" (TTC, 67)

"The vulgar people are pompous and flashy;
I alone look dull and dense.
The vulgar are clever and showy;
I alone am nebulous and in the dark...." (TTC, 20)

"Accordingly, when Tao is lost virtue arises;
When humanity is lost, morality arises;
When morality is lost, propriety arises.
Now propriety is the thinning-out of loyalty and trustworthiness,
And the beginning of disorder.
Those who have foreknowledge are [merely] the flower of Tao,
And the beginning of human folly.
Accordingly, the accomplished person holds to what is thick,
And does not reside in what is thin;
Holds to the fruit and does not reside in the flower.
Therefore, prefers the one and avoids the other." (TTC, 38)

"When the great Tao is abandoned,
There arises human morality;
When knowledge and cleverness appear,
There arises great hypocrisy;
When the six relationships[a] are in disharmony,
There arise 'filial piety' and 'parental affection';
When the state is in chaos,
'Loyal ministers' appear." (TTC, 18)

"Religion is a distortion." (HHC, 47)

Jesus: "...well did Isaiah prophesy about you when he said:

> *'This people honors me with their lips,*
> *but their hearts are far from me;*
> *in vain do they worship me,*
> *teaching as doctrines human precepts.'"*

He summoned the crowd and said to them, "Hear and understand. It is not what enters one's mouth that defiles that person; but what comes out of the mouth is what defiles one." "...the things that come out of the mouth come from the heart, and they defile. For from the heart come evil thoughts, murder, adultery, unchastity, theft, false witness, blasphemy. These are what defile a person, but to eat with unwashed hands does not defile." (Mt 15:7–20)

"Oh you Pharisees! Although you cleanse the outside of the cup and the dish, inside you are filled with plunder and evil. You fools! Did not the maker of the outside also make the inside? But as to what is within, give alms, and behold, everything will be clean for you. Woe to you Pharisees! You pay tithes of mint and of rue and of every garden herb, but you pay no attention to judgment and to love for God." (Lk 11:39–42)

"Woe to you, scribes and Pharisees, you hypocrites. You are like white-washed tombs, which appear beautiful on the outside, but inside are full of dead men's bones and every kind of filth. Even so, on the outside you appear righteous, but inside you are filled with hypocrisy and evildoing." (Mt 23:27–28)

---

[a] In Chinese tradition the six intimate relationships (*liu-ch'in*) refer to the bonds of parents, children, elder siblings, younger siblings, husbands, and wives.— Translators.

VACUOUS SUPERFICIALITY.

"The separation of intention and act is an artificial posture and does not accurately describe the human experience. "The act is in the intention, and the intention in the act," wrote Rollo May.[1] In the religious realm, outer forms of piety that contradict, hide, or betray inner intentions and attitudes are condemnable as artificial posturing.

Wu Ch'eng [1249–1333] interpreted the Tao as the fruit which, hanging from a tree, contains the power of life having its womb hidden. Once it falls, it puts forth virtue as its root, kindness as its stem, justice as its branches, rituals as its leaves, and knowledge as its flowers. The enlightened prefer the fruit to the leaves.[2]

NOTES.

INTRODUCTION.

1. Leo D. Lefebure, "Divergence, Convergence: Buddhist-Christian Encounters," *Christian Century* (October 16, 1996): 973. It is true that Lao Tzu and Chuang Tzu can be considered forerunners of Christ within a Christian patristic-style *semina verbi* theology that is experiencing somewhat of a revival in contemporary theological circles. This enables the great non-Christian religions and philosophical systems to be characterized as bearers of "seeds of the Word." Clearly, such theological co-opting is strictly an intramural exercise: more conducive to authentic Christian/non-Christian dialogue is the honest recognition and respect for the real differences that exist between the interested interlocutors. Cf. Claude Geffre, "La foi à l'age du pluralisme religieux," *La vie spirituelle* 143 (November–December 1989): 805–15.

2. Cf. Lee Yearley, "The Perfected Person in the Radical Chuang-tzu," in *Experimental Essays on Chuang Tzu,* ed., Victor H. Mair (Honolulu: University of Hawaii Press, 1983), 130–32.

3. Ashok K. Gangadean, "The Dialogical Revelution in Global Culture," in *Roundtable Anthology: Envisioning a Global Ethic,* resource text of the Consortium for Interreligious Dialogue Conference held at Haverford College (October 25, 1995), 1.

4. Ewert Cousins, "Judaism, Christianity, Islam: Facing Modernity Together," *Roundtable Anthology,* 6.

5. Leonard Swidler, *Roundtable Anthology,* 34.

6. Cousins, 20.

7. Ward Fellows, *Religions East and West* (New York: Holt, Rinehart and Winston, 1979), 245.

8. Ibid., 252–53.

9. Julia Ching and Hans Küng, *Christianity and Chinese Religions* (London: SCM Press Ltd., 1989), 132.

10. Ibid., 171.

11. Lewis M. Hopfe, *Religions of the World* (Westerville, Ohio: Glencoe Press, 1979), 169.

12. Leonard Swidler, *The Meaning of Life at the Edge of the Third Millennium* (New York: Paulist Press, 1992), 45–46.

13. Martin Heidegger, quoted by Küng in *Christianity and Chinese Religions,* 172.

14. Translations of the *Tao Te Ching* are taken from the unpublished work of Charles Wei-Hsun Fu and Susan A. Wawrytko.

15. Charles Wei-Hsun Fu, "Lao Tzu's Conception of Tao," *Inquiry* (Oslo, Norway: 1972): 19.

16. John B. Noss, *Man's Religions* (Indianapolis, Ind.: Macmillan, 1980), 252.

17. Ching and Küng, 178–79.

18. James Fredericks, "The Incomprehensibility of God: A Buddhist Reading of Aquinas," *Theological Studies* 56.3 (September, 1995): 520.

19. The phrasing of the questions of debate and the fundamental assumptions were adapted from the text, *Confessing Christian Faith in a Pluralistic Society* (Collegeville, Minn.: Institute for Ecumenical and Cultural Research, 1995): 4–11.

ABUNDANCE.

1. Thierry Maertens, O.S.B., *Bible Themes: A Source Book,* vol. I (Notre Dame, Ind.: Fides/Claretian, 1964), 301.

2. Peter K. H. Lee, "Nothingness and Fulfillment: From Laozi's Concept of *Wu* to Jesus' Teaching on the Kingdom of God," *Ching Feng* 29.2–3 (September, 1986): 125.

ACCEPTANCE.

1. Anthony de Mello, S.J., *Wellsprings: A Book of Spiritual Exercises* (New York: Image Books, Doubleday, 1986), 152.

2. Livia Kohn, *Taoist Mystical Philosophy: The Scripture of Western Ascension* (Albany: State University of New York Press, 1991), 54.

ACCOMPLISHMENT.

1. Cf. *The New Interpreter's Bible,* vol. 9, ed. Leander E. Keck (Nashville: Abingdon Press, 1995), 798.

2. Arthur Waley, *The Way and Its Power: A Study of the Tao Tê Ching and Its Place in Chinese Thought* (New York: Grove Press, 1958), 58–59.

3. Ellen M. Chen, *The Tao Te Ching: A New Translation with Commentary* (New York: Paragon House, 1989), 177.

ASCETICISM/MODERATION.

1. Robert Taft, S.J., *Beyond East and West: Problems in Liturgical Understanding* (Washington, D.C.: The Pastoral Press, 1984), 51–52.

2. Thomas Ryan, *Fasting Rediscovered* (Mahwah, N.J.: Paulist Press, 1981), 77, 131.

3. Red Pine, *Lao-Tzu's Taoteching, With Selected Commentaries of the Past 2000 Years* (San Francisco: Mercury House, 1996), 59.

AWARENESS.

1. From Julian of Norwich, *Revelation of Divine Love,* as quoted in Alfred Squire, *Asking the Fathers: The Art of Meditation and Prayer* (Mahwah, N.J.: Paulist Press, 1976), 174.

2. Agnes C. J. Lee, "Mahayana Teaching of No-Self and Christian Kenosis," *Ching Feng* 28.2–3 (August 1985): 147–48.

3. Agnes C. J. Lee, "Francis of Assisi and Chuang Tzu: A Comparative Study in Religious Consciousness," *Ching Feng* 28.2–3 (July 1984): 102.

CHILDLIKENESS.

1. Walter Burghardt, *Lovely in Eyes Not His* (Mahwah, N.J.: Paulist Press, 1988), 106.

2. From St. Francis de Sales, *Introduction to the Devout Life, Book III,* as quoted in Squire, 190.

3. E. M. Chen, 80, 187.

DARKNESS.

1. From John of the Cross, *Ascent of Mount Carmel,* as quoted in Squire, 207.

2. William Johnston, *The Inner Eye of Love: Mysticism and Religion* (London: Collins, 1978), 116–17.

3. Peter K. H. Lee, "Nothingness and Fulfillment: From Laozi's Concept of *Wu* to Jesus' Teaching on the Kingdom of God," *Ching Feng* 29.2–3 (September 1986): 126.

DISINTERESTED VIRTUE.

1. Archbishop Anthony Bloom, *Meditations: A Spiritual Journey Through the Parables* (Denville, N. J.: Dimension Books, 1971), 98–99.
2. Red Pine, 77.

EMPTY WORDS.

1. Frederick Buechner, *Wishful Thinking: A Theological ABC* (New York: Harper and Row, 1973), 96.
2. Quoted in Parker J. Palmer, *To Know As We Are Known: A Spirituality of Education* (San Francisco: Harper, 1983), 41.
3. St. Isaac of Syria, quoted in *Early Fathers from the Philokalia,* eds. E. Kadloubovsky and G. E. H. Palmer, (London: Faber and Faber, 1973), 198.

FLORA IMAGERY.

1. Wilfred J. Harrington, O.P., *A Key to the Parables* (Mahwah, N.J.: Paulist Press, 1964), 56.
2. E. M. Chen, 41. Chen, in her original translation, noted on page 15 of this text, provides these TTC citations:
    a. "Yielding" (first reference in the Chen extract), 76.1.
    b. "Yielding" (second reference), 16.2.
    c. "Perishing," 16.2.
    d. "Root," 6.2.
    e. "Spring," 40.2.
    f. "Return," 34.3.
    g. "Spring," 25.2.
    h. "Hard," 76.1.
    i. "Kingdom," 16.2.
3. Liu I-Ming, *Awakening to the Tao: Liu I-Ming,* trans. Thomas Cleary, (Boston: Shambhala, 1988), 31.

THE GREAT UNKNOWABLE/UNNAMEABLE.

1. Pseudo-Dionysius, *The Celestial Hierarchy,* quoted by Paul Rorem, "The Uplifting Spirituality of Pseudo-Dionysius," in *Christian Spirituality: Origins to*

the Twelfth Century, eds. Bernard McGinn and John Meyendorff (New York: Crossroad, 1988), 135.

    2. Wing-Tsit Chan, *The Way of the Tao* (Indianapolis: Bobbs-Merrill Co., Inc., 1963), 157.

GROUND OF BEING.

    1. John Macquarrie, *Principles of Christian Theology* (New York: Charles Scribner's Sons, 1966), 103–8.

    2. E. M. Chen, 179.

    3. Mary Carmen Rose, "The Maximal Mysticism of Bonaventure," *Anglican Theological Review* 58 (January 1976): 67–68.

"INJUSTICE" RESOLVED.

    1. Thomas Hopko, *All the Fullness of God: Essays on Orthodoxy, Ecumenism and Modern Society* (Crestwood, N. Y.: St. Vladimir's Seminary Press, 1982), 173–74.

    2. E. M. Chen, 123.

INTERIORITY.

    1. Thomas N. Hart, *The Art of Christian Listening* (Mahwah, N.J.: Paulist Press, 1980), 76.

    2. Huston Smith, *The World's Religions* (Harper San Francisco, 1991), 198.

LEADERSHIP.

    1. Michael R. Carey, "Transformative Christian Leadership," *Human Development* 12.1 (Spring 1991): 30.

    2. Waley, 166.

    3. Michael LaFargue, *The Tao of the Tao Te Ching: A Translation and Commentary* (Albany: State University of New York Press, 1992), 121.

    4. Red Pine, 132–33.

5. Ku-ying Ch'en, *Lao Tzu: Text, Notes and Comments,* translated and adapted by Rhett Y. W. Young and Roger T. Ames (San Francisco: Chinese Materials Center, Inc., 1977), 139.

LIBERATING THE OPPRESSED.

1. James W. Douglas, *Resistance and Contemplation: The Way of Liberation* (New York: Doubleday and Co., Inc., 1972), 77.
2. Red Pine, 154.
3. Ku-ying Ch'en, 302.

LIFESPRING.

1. Wing-Tsit Chan, 113.
2. E. M. Chen, 75.
3. Red Pine, 16–17.
4. LaFargue, 17.

LIGHT IMAGERY.

1. Robert J. Schreiter, C.P.P.S., "Light," *The Collegeville Pastoral Dictionary of Biblical Theology,* Carroll Stuhlmueller, C.P., et al., eds., (Collegeville, Minn.: Liturgical Press, 1996), 563.
2. Red Pine, 86.
3. *The Book of Balance and Harmony,* trans. Thomas Cleary (San Francisco: North Point Press, 1989), 5.
4. Liu I-Ming, 33.
5. Harold F. Oshima, "A Metaphorical Analysis of the Concept of Mind in the *Chuang-tzu,*" *Experimental Essays on Chuang Tzu,* ed. Victor H. Mair (Honolulu: University of Hawaii Press, 1983), 78.

LIMITLESSNESS.

1. E. M. Chen, 138.

LOVE OF SELF, OTHERS.

1. Quoted in Peter Nguyen Van Hai, "Synthesis of Christian Doctrine Through Cognitive Mapping," *Compass* 29.4 (Summer 1995): 36.
2. Joseph Needham, "The Tao—Illuminations and Corrections of the Way," *Theology* 81 (July, 1978): 252.
3. Chung-yuan Chang, *Tao: A New Way of Thinking: A Translation of the Tao Te Ching with an Introduction and Commentaries* (New York: Harper and Row, 1975), 181.

MEEKNESS/HUMILITY.

1. Michael Coogan, *The Oxford Companion to the Bible,* eds. Bruce M. Metzger and Michael Coogan (New York: Oxford University Press, 1993), 510.
2. *Philokalia,* 214–15.
3. From St. Francis de Sales, *Introduction to the Devout Life, Book III,* as quoted in Squire, 190.
4. Red Pine, 133.
5. Ibid., 99.
6. Smith, 211.

NONATTACHMENT.

1. "Matthew," in the *Anchor Bible,* eds. W. F. Albright and C. S. Mann (New York: Doubleday and Co., 1971), 233.
2. Margaret R. Miles, "Detachment," *Westminster Dictionary of Christian Spirituality,* ed. Gordon S. Wakefield (Philadelphia: Westminster Press, 1983), 111.
3. *Philokalia,* 172.
4. Lee Yearly, "The Perfected Person in the Radical Chuang Tzu," *Experimental Essays On Chuang Tzu,* 134–35.
5. LaFargue, 43.

NONCONFORMITY.

1. *Anchor Bible Dictionary,* vol. 5, ed. David Noel Freedman (New York: Doubleday and Co., 1992), 855.

2. Red Pine, 143.

NONCONTENTION/PACIFISM.

1. Daniel A. Dombrowski, *Christian Pacifism* (Philadelphia: Temple University Press, 1991), 125.
2. Ch'en Ku-ying, 293.
3. Red Pine, 16.

NONEXCLUSIVENESS.

1. Arnold Yeung, "Union with Tao in Tao te ching: A Dialogue between a Taoist and a Christian," *Dialogue and Alliance* (Spring 1991): 78.

NONJUDGMENT.

1. *Philokalia,* 163.
2. Alan K. L. Chan, *Two Visions of the Way: A Study of Wang Pi and the Ho-shang Kung Commentaries on the Lao-Tzu* (Albany: State University of New York Press, 1991), 54.

NONREVENGE.

1. Jurgen Moltmann, "Political Theology and the Ethics of Peace," *Theology, Politics and Peace,* ed. Theodore Runyon (Maryknoll, N. Y.: Orbis Books, 1989), 39–40.
2. E. M. Chen, 201–202.
3. Holmes Welch, *Taoism: The Parting of the Way,* rev. ed. (Boston: Beacon Press, 1965), 21.

NONVIOLENCE.

1. Thomas Merton, "Blessed Are the Meek: The Roots of Christian Nonviolence," *The Universe Bends Toward Justice: A Reader on Christian Nonviolence*

171

in the U.S., ed. Angie O'Gorman (Philadelphia: New Society Publishers, 1990), 199–200.

2. Lisa Sowle Cahill, *Love Your Enemies: Discipleship, Pacifism, and Just War Theory* (Minneapolis: Fortress Press, 1994), 246.

3. Ku-ying Ch'en, 282, 170.

NONWORRY.

1. E. M. Chen, 178.

ON LIFE, DEATH, AND THE LOGIC OF REVERSION.

1. *Philokalia,* 384.

OUTREACH.

1. Regis Duffy, O.F.M., *Real Presence: Worship, Sacraments, and Commitment* (San Francisco: Harper and Row, 1982), 151.

2. Red Pine, 17.

PEACEMAKERS.

1. Henri J. M. Nouwen, *Pray to Live* (Notre Dame, Ind.: Fides Publishers, Inc., 1972), 35–36. See "Nonviolence."

2. Paul Minear, "The Peace of God: Conceptions of Peace in the New Testament," *Celebrating Peace,* ed. Leroy S. Rouner (Notre Dame, Ind.: University of Notre Dame Press, 1990), 128–29.

3. LaFargue, 21.

PRACTICAL WISDOM.

1. Notes introducing the Wisdom Books, *New American Bible,* St. Joseph edition (New York: Catholic Book Publishing Co., 1970), 571.

2. Roland Murphy, O. Carm., "Wisdom," *The Collegeville Pastoral Dictionary of Biblical Theology,* 1084.

3. Red Pine, 39.

4. Red Pine, 129.

PERFECTION/UNITY/WHOLENESS.

1. *The New Interpreter's Bible,* vol. 8, 196.

2. *Westminster Dictionary of Christian Spirituality,* 299.

3. *Belief and Belonging: Living and Celebrating the Faith,* a catechetical text composed by the Catholic Bishops Conference of Belgium (Collegeville, Minn.: Liturgical Press, 1990), 215.

4. *Philokalia,* 212–213.

5. Ibid., 295.

6. Jennifer DeWeerth, "Perfection, Righteousness and Justice in the Sermon on the Mount," *Criterion,* 35.1 (Winter, 1996): 24.

7. Yu-lan Fung, *Chuang-Tzu: A New Selected Translation with an Exposition of the Philosophy of Kuo Hsiang* (Beijing: Foreign Languages Press, 1989), 136.

REPUDIATION OF POWER.

1. James W. Douglass, *Resistance and Contemplation: The Way of Liberation* (New York: Doubleday, 1972), 71.

2. Holmes Welch, *Taoism: The Parting of the Way,* 38–39.

3. LaFargue, 241–42.

REPUTATION.

1. Isaias Powers, *Quiet Places with Jesus: Forty Guided Imagery Meditations for Personal Prayer* (Mystic, Conn.: Twenty-Third Publications, 1988), 72.

2. Holmes Welch, 41.

RESPONSIBILITY FOR SELF.

1. Scott Peck, *Further Along the Road Less Traveled: The Unending Journey Toward Spiritual Growth* (New York: Simon and Schuster, 1993), 97.

2. Ku-ying Ch'en, 242–43.
3. *The Book of Balance and Harmony,* 15.

SEEKING/FINDING.

1. Joyce Rupp, *May I Have This Dance?* (Notre Dame, Ind.: Ave Maria Press, 1992), 86–87.

SELF AS NO-THING.

1. Quoted in Joseph M. Powers, *Spirit and Sacrament: The Humanizing Experience* (New York: Seabury Press, 1973), 13.
2. Powers, 15–16.
3. E. M. Chen, 161.

SELFLESSNESS.

1. Jerome Kodell, O.S.B., "Self-Denial," *The Collegeville Pastoral Dictionary of Biblical Theology* (New York: Catholic Book Publishing Co., 1970), 264.
2. Thomas Cleary, *The Essential Tao: An Initiation into the Heart of Taoism Through the Authentic Tao Te Ching and the Inner Teachings of Chuang-tzu,* (San Francisco: Harper San Francisco, 1991), 162.
3. *Awakening the Tao,* 28.

SOLICITUDE.

1. Cf. *The New Dictionary of Theology,* eds. Joseph A. Komonchak, Mary Collins, and Dermont A. Lane (Wilmington, Del.: Michael Glazier Inc., 1987), 816.
2. Red Pine, 102–3.

SOLITUDE/INWARDNESS.

1. Wilkie Au, S.J., and Noreen Cannon, C.S.J., "From Codependency to Contemplation," *Human Development* 12.2 (Summer 1991): 12.

2. From John of the Cross, *The Dark Night of the Soul,* as quoted in Squire, 196.

3. Palmer, 124.

4. Wu Yi, *Xin Yi Loa Tzu Jei Yi* (New Translation and Commentary on Lao Tzu), trans. by Wan-Li Ho (Taipei: San-Min Press, 1995), 371–72.

5. John Blofeld, *Taoism: The Road to Immortality* (Boston: Shambhala, 1985), 56–57.

STILLNESS/REST/TRANQUILITY.

1. Footnotes, Heb 3:7 to 4:13, *New American Bible,* St. Joseph edition, 341.

2. *Philokalia,* 38.

3. Red Pine, 101.

4. Words ascribed to Kuan-yin, associate of Lao Tzu, quoted in A. C. Green, "Taoist Spontaneity and the Dichotomy of 'Is' and 'Ought,'" *Experimental Essays on Chuang-tzu,* 10.

5. John Blofeld, *Taoism: The Road to Immortality,* 11.

STORYTELLING.

1. Richard Rohr, O.F.M., "The Goal of Christian Ministry," *The Catholic World* (September/October, 1994): 209.

2. Robert Allinson, *Chuang-Tzu For Spiritual Transformation: An Analysis of the Inner Chapters* (Albany: State University of New York Press, 1989), 23ff.

SUSTENANCE.

1. E. M. Chen, 140.

2. William Barklay, *The Gospel of Matthew,* vol. 1 (Philadelphia: Westminster Press, 1975), 68.

THE TAUGHT.

1. Red Pine, 108.

2. Ibid., 108.

3. Yi Wu, 415–16. Translated by Wan-Li Ho.

THE TEACHER (I).

1. Yi Wu, 172. Translated by Wan–Li Ho.

THE TEACHER (II).

1. Thomas Merton, *Mystics and Zen Masters* (New York: Farrar, Straus and Giroux, 1967), 76.

THE TEACHINGS.

1. LaFargue, 99.
2. Chung-yuan Chang, 186.
3. Red Pine, 140–141.
4. Ibid., 141.
5. E. M. Chen, 214.
6. Yi Wu, 504. Translated by Wan–Li Ho.

THE THREAT OF UNCHECKED DESIRES.

1. Cf. Tomas Spidlik, S.J., *The Spirituality of the Christian East: A Systematic Handbook* (Kalamazoo, Mich.: Cisterian Publications, 1986), 267–81.
2. Red Pine, 74.

UNITY OF FOCUS.

1. Thomas Merton, *No Man Is an Island* (New York: Harcourt Brace, 1955), 55-56.
2. Red Pine, 111.

UNITY OF OPPOSITES.

1. Edward Schillebeeckx, *Jesus, An Experiment in Christology* (New York: The Seabury Press, 1979), 340.

2. Chung-yuan Chang, 57.

3. Kristofer Shipper, *The Taoist Body,* trans. Karen C. Duval (Berkeley: University of California Press, 1993), 186–87.

VACUOUS SUPERFICIALITY.

1. Rollo May, *Love and Will* (New York: W. W. Norton, 1969), 230.

2. Red Pine, 77.

SOURCES LIST.

Allinson, Robert. *Chuang-Tzu for Spiritual Transformation: An Analysis of the Inner Chapters.* Albany: State University of New York Press, 1989.

The Anchor Bible. Edited by W. F. Albright and C. S. Mann. New York: Doubleday, 1971. S.v. "Matthew."

The Anchor Bible Dictionary. Edited by David Noel Freedman. New York: Doubleday, 1992.

Asking the Fathers: The Art of Meditation. Edited by Alfred Squire. Mahwah, N.J.: Paulist Press, 1976.

Au, Wilkie, and Noreen Cannon. "From Codependency to Contemplation." *Human Development* 12, no. 2 (Summer 1991): 12–15.

Barklay, William. *The Gospel of Matthew.* Vol. 1. Philadelphia: Westminster Press, 1975.

Blofeld, John. *Taoism: The Road to Immortality.* Boston: Shambhala, 1985.

Bloom, Anthony. *Meditations: A Spiritual Journey Through the Parables.* Denville, N.J.: Dimension Books, 1971.

The Book of Balance and Harmony. Translated by Thomas Cleary. San Francisco: North Point Press, 1989.

Buechner, Frederick. *Wishful Thinking: A Theological ABC.* New York: Harper and Row, 1973.

Burghardt, Walter. *Lovely in Eyes Not His.* Mahwah, N.J.: Paulist Press, 1988.

Cahill, Lisa Sowle. *Love Your Enemies: Discipleship, Pacifism, and Just War Theory.* Minneapolis: Fortress Press, 1994.

Carey, Michael R. "Transformative Christian Leadership." *Human Development* 12, no. 1 (Spring 1991): 30–34.

Catholic Bishops Conference of Belgium. *Belief and Belonging: Living and Celebrating the Faith.* Collegeville, Minn.: Liturgical Press, 1986.

Catholic Study Bible. New York: Oxford University Press, 1990.

Celebrating Peace. Edited by Leroy S. Rouner. Notre Dame, Ind.: University of Notre Dame Press, 1990.

Chan, Alan K.L. *Two Visions of the Way: A Study of Wang Pi and the Ho-shang Kung Commentaries on the Lao-Tzu.* Albany: State University of New York Press, 1991.

Chan, Wing-Tsit. *The Way of the Tao.* Indianapolis: Bobbs-Merrill, 1963.

Chang, Chung-yuan. *Tao—A New Way of Thinking: A Translation of the Tao Te Ching with an Introduction and Commmentaries.* New York: Harper and Row, 1975.

Ch'en, Ku-ying. *Lao Tzu: Text, Notes and Comments.* Translated and adapted by Rhett Y. M. Young and Roger T. Ames. San Francisco: Chinese Materials Center, 1977.

Chen, Ellen M. *The Tao Te Ching: A New Translation with Commentary.* New York: Paragon House, 1989.

Ching, Julia, and Hans Küng. *Christianity and Chinese Religions.* London: SCM Press Ltd, 1989.

Cleary, Thomas. *The Essential Tao: An Initiation into the Heart of Taoism Through the Authentic Tao Te Ching and the Inner Teachings of Chuang-tzu.* San Francisco: Harper San Francisco, 1991.

The Collegeville Pastoral Dictionary of Biblical Theology. Edited by Carroll Stuhlmueller et al. Collegeville, Minn.: Liturgical Press, 1996.

Confessing Christian Faith in a Pluralistic Society. Collegeville, Minn.: Institute for Ecumenical and Cultural Research, 1995.

de Mello, Anthony. *Wellsprings: A Book of Spiritual Exercises.* New York: Doubleday, 1989.

DeWeerth, Jennifer. "Perfection, Righteousness and Justice in the Sermon on the Mount." *Criterion* 35, no. 1 (Winter 1996): 23-25.

Dombrowski, Daniel A. *Christian Pacifism.* Philadelphia: Temple University Press, 1991.

Douglass, James W. *Resistance and Contemplation: The Way of Liberation.* New York: Doubleday, 1972.

Duffy, Regis. *Real Presence: Worship, Sacraments, and Commitment.* San Francisco: Harper and Row, 1982.

Experimental Essays on Chuang Tzu. Edited by Victor H. Mair. Honolulu: University of Hawaii Press, 1983.

Fellows, Ward. *Religions East and West.* New York: Holt, Rinehart and Winston, 1979.

Fredericks, James. "The Incomprehensibility of God: A Buddhist Reading of Aquinas." *Theological Studies* 56, no. 3 (September 1995): 506–20.

Fu, Charles Wei-Hsun. *Inquiry.* Oslo, Norway: 1972.

Fung, Yu-lan. *Chuang-Tzu: A New Selected Translation with an Exposition of the Philosophy of Kuo Hsiang.* Beijing: Foreign Language Press, 1989.

Geffre, Claude. "La foi à l'age du pluralisme religieux." *La vie Spirituelle* 143 (November–December 1989): 805–15.

Harrington, Wilfred J. *A Key to the Parables.* Mahwah, N.J.: Paulist Press, 1964.

Hart, Thomas N. *The Art of Christian Listening.* Mahwah, N.J.: Paulist Press, 1980.

Hopfe, Lewis M. *Religions of the World.* Westerville, Ohio: Glencoe Press, 1979.

Hopko, Thomas. *All the Fullness of God: Essays on Orthodoxy, Ecumenism and Modern Society.* Crestwood, N.Y.: St. Vladimir's Seminary Press, 1982.

Kadloubovsky, E. and G. E. H. Palmer, eds. and trans. *Early Fathers from the Philokalia.* London: Faber and Faber, 1973.

Kohn, Livia. *Taoist Mystical Philosophy: The Scripture of Western Ascension.* Albany: State University of New York Press, 1991.

LaFargue, Michael. *The Tao of the Tao Te Ching: A Translation and Commentary.* Albany: State University of New York Press, 1992.

Lee, Agnes C. J. "Francis of Assisi and Chuang Tzu: A Comparative Study in Religious Consciousness." *Ching Feng* 28, no. 2–3 (July 1984): 94–114.

Lee, Agnes C. J. "Mahayana Teaching of No-Self and Christian Kenosis." *Ching Feng* 28, no. 2–3 (August 1985): 130–151.

Lee, Peter K. H. "Christianized Hsin-Hsing Spirituality." *Ching Feng* 28, no. 2–3 (July 1984): 73–93.

Lee, Peter K. H. "Nothingness and Fulfillment: From Laozi's Concept of *Wu* to Jesus' Teaching on the Kingdom of God." *Ching Feng* 29, no. 2–3 (September 1986): 106–28.

Lefebure, Leo D. "Divergence, Convergence: Buddhist-Christian Encounters." *Christian Century* 113, no. 29 (October 16, 1996): 964–73.

Liu, I-Ming. *Awakening to the Tao: Liu I-Ming.* Translated by Thomas Cleary. Boston: Shambhala, 1988.

Macquarrie, John. *Principles of Christian Theology.* New York: Charles Scribner's Sons, 1966.

Maertens, Thierry. *Bible Themes: A Source Book.* Vol. 1. Notre Dame, Ind.: Fides/Claretian, 1964.

May, Rollo. *Love and Will.* New York: W. W. Norton, 1969.

Merton, Thomas. *Mystics and Zen Masters.* New York: Farrar, Straus and Giroux, 1967.

Merton, Thomas. *No Man Is an Island.* New York: Harcourt Brace, 1955.

Moltmann, Jurgen. "Political Theology and the Ethics of Peace." In *Theology, Politics and Peace,* 39–40. Edited by Theodore Runyon. Maryknoll, N.Y.: Orbis Books, 1989.

Needham, Joseph. "The Tao—Illuminations and Corrections of the Way." *Theology* 81 (July 1978): 244–52.

New American Bible. St. Joseph's Edition. New York: Catholic Book Publishing Co., 1970.

The New Dictionary of Theology. Edited by Joseph A. Komonchak, Mary Collins, and Dermont A. Lane. Wilmington, Del.: Michael Glazier, 1987.

New Interpreter's Bible. Vols. 8 and 9. Edited by Leander Keck. Nashville: Abingdon Press, 1995.

Noss, John B. *Man's Religions.* Indianapolis: Macmillan, 1980.

Nouwen, Henri J. M. *Pray to Live.* Notre Dame, Ind.: Fides Publishers, 1972.

The Oxford Companion to the Bible. Edited by Bruce M. Metzger and Michael Coogan. New York: Oxford University Press, 1993, 510.

Palmer, Parker J. *To Know As We Are Known: A Spirituality of Education.* San Francisco: Harper San Francisco, 1983.

Peck, Scott. *Further Along the Road Less Traveled: The Unending Journey Toward Spiritual Growth.* New York: Simon and Schuster, 1993.

Powers, Isaias. *Quiet Places with Jesus: Forty Guided Imagery Meditations for Personal Prayer.* Mystic, Conn.: Twenty-Third Publications, 1988.

Powers, Joseph M. *Spirit and Sacrament: The Humanizing Experience.* New York: Seabury Press, 1973.

Pseudo-Dionysius. *The Celestial Hierarchy.* Quoted in Paul Rorem. "The Uplifting Spirituality of Pseudo-Dionysius." In *Christian Spirituality: Origins to the Twelfth Century,* 132–51. Edited by Bernard McGinn, John Meyendorff and Jean Leclerq. New York: Crossroad, 1988.

Red Pine. *Lao-Tzu's Taoteching: With Selected Commentaries of the Past 2000 Years.* San Francisco: Mercury House, 1996.

Rohr, Richard. "The Goal of Christian Ministry." *The Catholic World* 237, no. 1421 (September/October 1994): 204–9.

Rose, Mary Carmen. "The Maximal Mysticism of Bonaventure." *Anglican Theological Review* 58 (January 1976): 60–75.

Roundtable Anthology: Envisioning a Global Ethic. Delaware Valley Consortium for Interreligious Dialogue, 1995: 1–8.

Rupp, Joyce. *May I Have This Dance?* Notre Dame, Ind.: Ave Maria Press, 1992.

Ryan, Thomas. *Fasting Rediscovered.* Mahwah, N.J.: Paulist Press, 1981.

Schillebeeckx, Edward. *Jesus, An Experiment in Christology.* New York: Seabury Press, 1979.

Shipper, Kristoffer. *The Taoist Body.* Translated by Karen C. Duval. Berkeley: University of California Press, 1993.

Squire, Alfred. *Asking the Fathers: The Art of Meditation and Prayer.* Mahwah, N.J.: Paulist Press, 1976.

Smith, Huston. *The World's Religions.* San Francisco: Harper San Francisco, 1991.

Spidlik, Tomas. *The Spirituality of the Christian East: A Systematic Handbook.* Kalamazoo, Mich.: Cistercian Publications, 1986.

Swidler, Leonard. *The Meaning of Life at the Edge of the Third Millennium.* Mahwah, N.J.: Paulist Press, 1992.

Taft, Robert. *Beyond East and West: Problems in Liturgical Undrstanding.* Washington, D.C.: Pastoral Press, 1984.

The Universe Bends Toward Justice: A Reader on Christian Nonviolence in the U.S. Edited by Angie O'Gorman. Philadelphia: New Society Publishers, 1990.

Van Hai, Peter Nguyen. "Synthesis of Christian Doctrine Through Cognitive Mapping." *Compass* 29, no. 4 (Summer 1995): 36.

Waley, Arthur. *The Way and Its Power: A Study of the Tao Tê Ching and Its Place in Chinese Thought.* New York: Grove Press, 1958.

Welch, Holmes. *Taoism: The Parting of the Way.* Boston: Beacon Press, 1965.

Westminster Dictionary of Christian Spirituality. Edited by Gordon S.
   Wakefield. Philadelphia: Westminster Press, 1983.

Wu, Yi. *Xin Yi Lao Tzu Jei Yi: New Translation and Commentary on Lao
   Tzu.* Translated by Wan Li Ho. Taipei: San-Min Press, 1995.

Yeung, Arnold. "Union with Tao in Tao te ching: A Dialogue between a
   Taoist and a Christian." *Dialogue and Alliance* 5, no. 1 (Spring
   1991): 68–80.